play it!

Over 150 great games for youth groups

The best of
Play It! and
Play It Again!
in one volume!

play it!

Over 150 great games for youth groups

Wayne Rice and Mike Yaconelli

Youth Specialties

ZondervanPublishingHouse
Grand Rapids, Michigan

A Division of HarperCollinsPublishers

Play It! Over 150 great games for youth groups

Copyright © 2000 by Youth Specialties

Youth Specialties Books, 300 S. Pierce St., El Cajon, CA 92020, are published by Zondervan
Publishing House, 5300 Patterson Ave. SE, Grand Rapids, MI 49530.

Library of Congress Cataloging-in-Publication Data

Play it! : over 150 great games for youth groups : the best of Play it! and Play it again! in
one volume! / [edited by] Wayne Rice & Mike Yaconelli.
     p. cm.
Includes index.
ISBN 0-310-23629-0
   1. Group games. 2. Cooperativeness. I. Rice, Wayne. II. Yaconelli, Mike. III. Play it
again!

GV1201 .P53 2000
790.1'5—dc21

                                               00-043412

Edited by David Lambert, J. Cheri McLaughlin, Lory Floyd, and Mary Fletcher
Cover and interior design by Razdezignz

Printed in the United States of America

  01 02 03 04 05 06 / / 10 9 8 7 6 5 4

Contents

Play it!

Alphabetical list of games

Play It! again...and again

Who doesn't love games? Those who teach or work with children, middle schoolers, high schoolers–hey, even adults–know the value of group games and activities for building community, establishing a sense of team, and simply having fun.

And this is no ordinary game book. This newly revised version of *Play It!* is a collection of the greatest games from the original best-sellers *Play It!* and *Play It Again!*–originally published in 1986 and 1993. The games in these books have been a valuable resource for thousands of youth workers, Sunday school teachers, camp counselors, activity coordinators, and parents–who've needed an easy-to-use collection of group games.

So for all of those who thrive on game books, here is a new version of over 150 great games for youth groups (or just about any other kinds of groups you may have!). The games in this book originally appeared in the Ideas Library (Youth Specialties) and all are reprinted by permission. Thanks to all of the creative youth workers who originally developed these games and who contributed them for publication.

Play It! contains only games that have potential to build community–most have nothing to do with winning or with skill. These games are simply fun and they're playable by nearly everyone. And there's no emphasis on competition–yes, good games are competitive–but competition can hurt groups by driving wedges between the "good" and "bad" players or the "skilled" and the "nonskilled." Participation is important! So be sure to get everyone involved (even those standing on the side, scared of being ridiculed or embarrassed!). The goal of these games is to build community within your group, without focusing on the competition.

Choosing the games

There are over 120 games in this book, so you don't have to worry about finding a game that's right for your situation. There are more games here than you'll probably ever need. But how do you decide which game is the right game to play? Here are some elements to consider when searching for a game for your group–

Safety. Of course, any game can result in an accidental injury, but sometimes people are hurt because precautions aren't taken. When you present a game to others, they assume you've taken every precaution for their safety. Here are some safety suggestions for any game you play–

- Make sure that you've played—or at least thought through—any game that you decide to use.
- Take extra precautions when playing with small children or elderly adults.
- Check the playing area for protruding objects, hard surfaces, obstacles, slippery floors,

or other hazards that could hurt the players.

- If you change or adapt a game, think through how the changes could affect the safety of players.
- Encourage the more athletic players in your group to not dominate the game by being too aggressive. If some continue to play roughly, give them some kind of handicap, such as hopping on one leg or using only their left hands.
- Double check your insurance coverage to make sure injuries are covered adequately.
- Always have adequate first-aid equipment on hand.
- When you sponsor a large, day-long game event with young people, require parental release forms permitting immediate care to be given to players who might be injured.

Age of group. The games in this book can be played by people of all ages, but some games are better for certain groups. For example, cooperative games that require little physical contact work best with families, but high school guys enjoy high-energy games with lots of physical contact.

Sex. You may want to separate the guys and girls for some games. Although girls often enjoy playing physical, hard-hitting games too, it's important to consider the consequences of certain types of physical play and plan accordingly.

Group size. Consider how a game will work with the size of your group. Games like Ultimate Elimination (page 17) don't work well with a small group, but games like Tarzan Kickball (page 23) work fine.

Personality. Every group has a unique personality. Some groups are active, outgoing or physical, while others are more easygoing or sedentary. It's good to give a group new experiences, but it's also good to start with a game that the group feels comfortable playing. Choose games that your group will enjoy.

Ability. Think of your group's ability when planning. Some people have trouble doing certain actions. For example, young children have a hard time balancing cups of water on their heads while older people may have trouble hopping around a football field.

Include everyone in your game playing. Chose carefully when your group contains people with physical or mental disabilities. Encourage those who don't want to play to participate as referees, game photographers, or scorekeepers.

Purpose. Besides building community and having fun, games are good for many reasons—wearing out restless campers on the first and last nights of camp, helping people become better acquainted, or providing exercise. Let your purpose influence the game choice, too.

Adapting the games

Games can be played anywhere, anytime, with anyone. Any game can be adapted to fit any set of circumstances. Here are some tips for adapting the-

Rules. Rules tell you how to play a game, but that doesn't mean you can't play it a different way. Feel free to adapt the rules to make the game better. For example, if your group is playing baseball and no one can hit the ball because the pitching is too fast, make a rule that pitches have to be underhand slow. Adapt the rules so the game is fun.

Time. Feel free to interrupt or shorten the game if it isn't going well-maybe your group is bored, tired, or not interested in playing. But you may want to lengthen the game if everyone is having fun.

Weather. You can't change the weather, but you can adapt a game to the weather. If it's raining, play volleyball in the rain, play volleyball in raincoats or play mud volleyball. Bad weather, within reason (avoid hail and lightning!), doesn't have to stop a game.

Equipment. Some games require equipment-but you aren't a slave to equipment. If you can't find a volleyball, use a soccer ball, four-square ball, two tee shirts wadded up, or maybe a grapefruit. And if what you find affects the outcome of the game, change the rules.

Explaining the rules

It's important that you explain the basic rules of a game simply, clearly, and as quickly as possible. If your group doesn't understand the rules or instructions of the game, you'll have mass confusion. Have fun while explaining the game-you want to get your kids excited to play. To avoid all the what-if questions, you may want to demonstrate how the game is played or play a couple practice rounds before you start.

You must have everyone's attention when explaining the game. Don't ever try to shout direction to an inattentive group. Get the group's attention by sounding a good referee's whistle or marine boat horn. And it's a good idea to begin with this rule: Whenever the horn or whistle is blown, everyone must sit down and be quiet. You may want to use a bullhorn when instructing large groups.

Choosing teams

If a game requires teams, think of a way to automatically form groups. Consider dividing the group members into teams by their birthdays, color of clothing, cabin at camp, or favorite food. The quality of a team isn't determined by size, strength, or athletic ability. All you need for a good team is a group of people who want to play and are willing to have fun!

Referees

Every game requires people to help conduct and supervise, especially with large groups of players. A good ratio is one leader for every 20 players. When looking for volunteer referees, you'll find there are two types–the letter-of-the-law ref (who enforces the rules to the letter) and the fun-and-games ref (who understands that rules are nothing more than guidelines to make a game enjoyable). Encourage a happy medium–the games should be safe and fun.

Clearly identify the referees (maybe ask them to wear a fluorescent hat or a brightly colored shirt) and make sure that all the referees understand the rules of the game.

Points

Some groups use points to keep track of teams during game events. The amount of points you give can actually increase the enjoyment and excitement of those who are playing! Points are free, so you don't have to be stingy with them. Give lots of points—1000 points! 3000! After all, what group wants to play a game for 50 measly points when they can win 3000? Live a little! Give 10,000 points!

Have fun!

Now you can start doing what you're supposed to be doing—playing! May the games you play be fun and enjoyable, bring you closer to the people you play with, and help you rediscover the joy of playing games!

1

These games are geared for groups of 30 or more playing in wide-open spaces. No matter how large your group is or what limitations of terrain you face, you'll find contests and activities that will work for you.

Holy Man

The gurus in your group will love this hide-and-seek game, perfect for summer evenings. Select one of your teens to be the "Holy Man," who—dressed in an identifying robe or hat—takes a lit candle and hides somewhere within the boundaries of the game (although he can move around at will and hide somewhere new). When the Holy Man is settled, the other kids—each armed with a squirt gun and an unlit candle—spread out to find him.

When kids discover the Holy Man, they light their own candles from his and then, by stealth more than speed, try to get back to a designated home base before their candles are extinguished by others' squirt guns. (The Holy Man's candle cannot be extinguished by other players.) If their flames get doused, they must return to the Holy Man to relight their candles. The first player to arrive at home base with a lit candle is the winner.
Ann Smith

Field Handball

For this football-soccer hybrid, you'll need a large ball (soccer ball, football, volleyball—even a playground ball will do), two durable chairs, and tape or spray paint or rope to mark off the goal circles. Pylons to mark the field boundaries and armbands to distinguish teams are optional.

The goal of play is simply to hit the opponent's chair—which sits in the center of a 12-foot-diameter goal circle at the end of the field—with the ball.

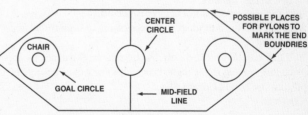

Here's how to play:
- You may run with the ball or pass the ball to a teammate.
- If a ball runner is tagged, she has three seconds to pass the ball to a teammate; otherwise, the other team takes possession on the spot. A goal cannot be scored during these three seconds.

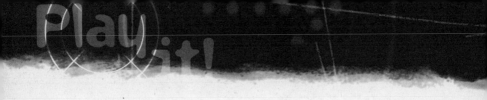

- If a player drops a pass from a teammate, any opponent picks up the ball and continues play. An intercepted pass is also played without a break.
- No one, defender or attacker, may enter either of the goal circles. Otherwise, the ball changes possession and play is renewed at the nearest boundary line.
- Following a goal, play begins again in the center circle as in soccer. You may want to use a referee, especially to curtail unnecessary roughness. The referee can impose a loss-of-possession penalty or temporary suspension from the game. *Mark E. Byers*

Hurl Hockey

With one or two dozen plastic gallon milk jugs, you can play a fast, fun court game that's a mix of hockey and jai alai.

Cut the bottom out of the jugs in order to make a "glove" that also can hurl a ball toward a goal (see diagram).

One way to create a goal for Hurl Hockey is to split a Ping-Pong table in half and set each half at one end of the court; the goal is below the mid-stripe. Use masking tape to mark off an eight-by-six-foot goalie box in front of each goal.

The game itself is played as hockey, though with a soft, baseball-size ball instead of a puck; the ball can be scooped off the floor with the plastic gloves and passed or hurled at the goal.

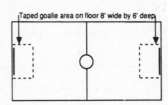
Taped goalie area on floor 8' wide by 6' deep

(Goal area is shaded)

Cut along dots

Here are other details:
- Start the game with a hockey-type face-off.
- With the ball in their gloves, players can take only three steps, then must pass it or shoot at the goal.
- The ball can be touched only by the plastic glove, not by feet or by a player's free hand.
- Traveling (taking more than three steps) or out-of-bounds results in the nearest goalie putting the ball back into play.

Paul Holmberg

Blind One-Legged Kickball

When other baseball-diamond games get old, try this variation: all fielders can move about only on one leg, flamingo style, and must throw with their "odd" arm (right-handers, for example, must throw with only their left arms). Furthermore, all kickers are blindfolded;

coaches stationed at each base yell out directions to their runners.

It's as hilarious to watch as to play—and it can easily become a discussion starter as well (our dependence on each other, trust, etc.). *Paul Bertelson*

Ultimate Elimination

If you have 30 or more kids and a big playing field, this game can continue for a long, exciting time. Students should pair off and tie themselves together at the arm. Throw into the fray several Frisbees, Nerf balls, playground balls, or a combination of them—and it's every pair for itself. When one person of a pair is hit, she can no longer throw, but can only defend her partner. When her partner is hit as well, that pair is out of the game altogether— that is, until the pair that finally eliminated them is itself eliminated. Then the first pair can join the game again.

Just when you think the game is winding down, a lethal pair that eliminated several other pairs is itself eliminated—and competition picks up quickly as those renewed pairs can play again. *Randy Hausler*

Pillow Hockey

The object of the game is to use pillowcases stuffed loosely with crumpled newspapers and tied off to hit, hockey fashion, a playground ball into a goal.

Lay the available pillows out on the court (an equal number on both sides of the court), then call for teams to select players, who run out to the court and immediately begin playing. When one side scores, call for new players from each team.

What makes this game fun is that it's difficult to hit the ball with much force, or even be too sure you hit it at all. Also, unlike Broom Hockey, players don't get smacked accidentally by wooden handles. *Keith King*

Inner Tube Baseball

This game is similar to softball, but it utilizes an inner tube. The batter picks up the inner tube at home plate and rotates seven times, heaving the inner tube into the field on the seventh rotation. The batter's team may count out loud as the batter rotates to help him or her keep track of when to release the tube. Although there are three bases as in softball, there is no out of bounds, so the inner tube may be released in any direction once seven rotations have been completed.

Players are only out when tagged with the inner tube. There are no force outs or pop flies.

Defensive players may tag a base runner by touching the runner with the tube or throwing the tube at the runner. Any time the base runner comes in contact with the tube, he is out (unless he is on base, of course).

There is one penalty in this game called "jamming." Jamming occurs when a defensive player tries to cream a base runner with the tube (unnecessary roughness). This is a judgment call on the part of the umpire. Award the offended team with a run and allow the base runner to advance to the closest base. Without this rule some players will attempt to start another game called Maul Ball, which is not recommended for most amateur Inner Tube Baseball players.

The last rule is that the umpire can add or subtract any rules at any time to make the game fun and exciting. All umpire rulings are final unless the umpire receives sufficient financial reimbursement, thus influencing the outcome of the game.

If you wish, have several sizes of inner tubes available so kids can choose a tube appropriate for their size. *Steve Smoker*

Buzzards And Eagles

Divide players into four teams and give them names like "Buzzards," "Eagles," "Turkeys," and other bird names. Then designate a headquarters for each team that is an equal distance from what will be called the "Central Nest." The object of the game is for each team to transport eggs from their headquarters to the Central Nest. Each egg is worth 1,000 points.

Give the teams an equal number of eggs—real ones or plastic, colored eggs. Each team will also need a portable nest—that is, a common bathroom plunger! Finally, every player needs a feather or a strip of cloth that is tucked into the waist as in flag football. Don't allow kids to tie them to their jeans or tuck them in so far that they're hidden.

Once a team has its eggs at its own headquarters, it may—on your signal—begin transporting them to the Central Nest, but only in the portable nest. Obviously, several trips back and forth will be required for each team, since the portable nest will only hold a few eggs.

Players may try to keep other teams from transporting their eggs by plucking them—that is, by pulling their flags, flag-football style. Anyone who is plucked must report to the bird hospital and see the vet for five minutes before returning to play.

If players pluck someone who is carrying a portable nest with eggs, they can take those eggs to their own headquarters and use them to score points for their team. However, players cannot steal another team's portable nest or break it. Players are also forbidden to enter another team's headquarters. To keep this game from getting too rough, you should rule out tackling or holding players down in order to pluck them.

Besides the score for eggs, you can award a team additional points each time they pluck someone. Just have the plucker and the pluckee report in.

If you're at camp with a large staff of counselors, designate them as buzzards, whose only job is to run around plucking eagles and to make them drop their eggs as they run for the Central Nest. (In this case, there would be only two teams.) *Teen Valley Ranch*

Toilet Tag

This version of tag brings a new flush to that time-worn game. Mark off the playing area suitable for your size group. Designate one or more players to be "It." Those who are "It" run around attempting to tag other players, who are then "dead" and must kneel down on one knee with one arm out and to the side. Dead players can reenter the game only when a free player sits on their knee and pulls down their hand—"flushes the toilet." The game ends when all the players except "It" are kneeling. *Randy Hausler*

Parachute Kickball

Mark off a 100-foot square in the church parking lot or in a field. Divide players into two teams. One team stands within the square, each helping to hold a parachute or large sheet. The other team stands outside the square, either scattered around it or together in a line; this team has a soccer or playground ball.

The object for the outside team is to take turns kicking the ball with a high, arching kick that lands within the square. If the ball lands within the square and is not caught by the parachute, the kicking team gets a point. If the ball is caught by the parachute, or if the kicked ball lands outside the square, or if the kick is judged to be insufficiently high or arching—then an out is called against the kicking team. As in baseball, teams trade places after three outs. *David Shaw*

Duckball

Try this game of kickball with a twist. The pitcher rolls the ball toward the kicker (a one-pitch limit if the group is large), and the kicker kicks away. Before he runs to first base, however, he's handed a fully inflated balloon that he must tuck between his knees, and keep there as long as he runs or is on base. Fielders, meanwhile, are also equipped with balloons between their knees (except the pitcher, who cannot assist his team at all) and must waddle as best they can to retrieve the ball and attempt to put the runners out.

Outs are made by touching runners with the ball, either by a tag or a throw. Overthrown balls limit a runner to a single base, as in baseball.

Points are scored by crossing home plate—but that's not the only way. If a fielder pops his balloon, the other team scores a point. Likewise, if a runner pops his balloon, the fielding team scores a point. The game ends when a team earns 10 points or when a predetermined number of innings have been played.

You'll need at least 50 to 60 balloons in a large plastic bag or trash can to begin the game. Use the kids who don't want to play to maintain the balloon supply and to hand balloons to runners on their way to first base.

Variation: If you play Duckball indoors, use a Nerf ball. *Michael W. Capps*

Kick Golf

No green fees for this round of golf. Set up your own nine-hole course: Hula Hoops are the greens, small sticks stuck within them are the flags, and small playground balls are the golf balls. Roll the ball against the stick, and consider it sunk.

For each hole, lay a marker to show where players tee-off. And don't forget to set par: Use hills and other obstacles to vary the difficulty of each hole. Distribute scorecards, and play by teams if you like. *Tammy Larkey and Julie D. Anderson*

Nonstop Cricket

I say, how 'bout a game of English nonstop cricket? Using the diagram to guide you, make a bat (or use a similar wooden paddle), make wickets from old broomsticks and a base block, and buy a foam ball. Form two teams of six to 11 participants—the fielders and the players. Choose a wicket keeper from the fielders and a score keeper from among nonplayers (or have a batter record the runs).

The bowler bowls (pitches) with an underhanded throw to the batter, aiming to hit the wicket.

- The batter attempts to hit the ball and on a hit must run and touch the scoring line and return to his crease, so scoring a run.
- The batter is out if the wicket is hit by the bowler, a bowl hits the leg of the batter in front of the wicket, the ball is returned by a fielder and hits the wicket before the batter returns to the crease, or the wicket keeper hits the wicket with the ball while the batter is out of the crease.
- The batter must run on

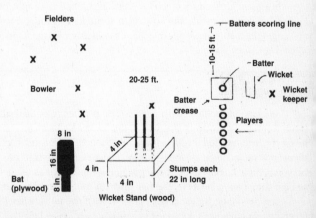

the third bowl or forfeit a turn.
- The playing field surrounds the batter's crease on all sides.
- Fielders attempt to hit the wicket with the ball directly or through the wicket keeper or bowler. The bowler can bowl whether the batter has returned to the crease or not.
- The entire batting team is out if a fielder catches a fly ball.

Otherwise the batters keep playing until the last batter is out. The batters then become the fielders, and the fielders become the batters. Play for a set time or until an agreed score is reached. *Fred Swallow*

Frisbee Bull's-Eye

Add this to an afternoon of Frisbee mania. This two-part game works best with 30 kids or more. Divide them into three or four teams, then announce the first part: competition in a stated game (it doesn't matter what game) in order to earn Frisbees. First place is awarded five Frisbees; second place, three Frisbees; third place, two; and fourth place, one.

Now for part two: Each team appoints a thrower, who is entrusted with floating his team's Frisbees onto a horizontal target from behind a line 20 feet or so away from the target. The target can simply be three concentric circles—throwers score 10 points for their team if a Frisbee lands within the innermost circle, five points within the next circle, and one point if within the outside circle.

Teams can play as many rounds of this as they like, giving most of a team's players the chance to be thrower. *Randy Hausler*

Time Warp Tag

Here's another crazy version of the most famous of all games. You simply play a regular game of tag but at the blow of a whistle, each player (including "It") must slow down to a speed equal to a sports replay "slo-mo." In other words, they must do everything in slow motion. Kids will soon get the hang of it and become very exaggerated in their motions.

Make sure the kids do everything in Time Warp state, even talking and shouting. The game can be played in total Time Warp, or you can blow the whistle for start/stop intervals. Limit the size of the playing area so that several players have a chance to become "It." *Mark A. Simone*

Play In The Dark

For nighttime football, make a hole in a Nerf ball and push a Cyalume glow stick into the end of the ball. Point the lighted end toward the receiver for passing downs. Or attach a Cyalume glow stick to a Frisbee to play Frisbee in the dark. *Larry Smith*

Missionary

In this game, each team must guide its missionary safely though a field of headhunters (the other team). You'll need to divide into two teams of equal size.

The first team, the missionaries, chooses one of its members to travel through a dangerous mission field. That player must put a paper bag over his head and move across the playing field from a starting line to a finish line while trying to avoid being touched by any of the headhunters. Teammates guide the missionary across the field by shouting directions to him, but they must coordinate the directions and shout them in unison to avoid confusion. Teammates cannot walk with the missionary.

Meanwhile, the other team, the headhunters, spreads out over the playing field. They will attempt to impede the progress of the missionary by touching him. They cannot, however, move from their original positions on the field, except once during each round, when they may take three giant steps in any direction. Any contact with the missionary must be made while a headhunter is standing still, so these steps must be planned carefully. The headhunters may also shout false instructions to the missionary, but silence is often a better strategy.

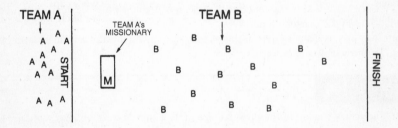

Each team has one chance to guide a missionary and one chance to be headhunters. The missionary is timed from the starting line to the finish line, with a penalty of 20 seconds added for every contact with a headhunter. The team with the lowest time wins. *Ray Wilson*

Lightning Strikes

For this game you need a dark night, a large open place like a football field or even an empty parking lot, a few old sheets or blankets, and a glow-ball—the kind that glows when you break a cylinder of fluorescent liquid and put it inside the ball. Divide into two teams, assign three to eight kids to a sheet, and align them within their own zones like this on the field:

Holding the edges of the sheet and quickly stretching it taut, a team uses it to fling the ball toward the goal at the end of the field. A team gets to fling the ball only when it lands in that team's zone. Goals are at opposite ends of the field, as in football, and each goal earns (why be stingy?—points are free) 10,000 points. Any throwing of the ball by hand, of course, earns 10,000 points for the other team.

The visual effect at night is neat—the eerie glow zips and zigs and zags through the darkness. With enough kids, you may want to use more than one ball. *David Washburn*

Velcro War

For this textile tag game, go to a craft store and purchase golf-ball-size plastic balls and Velcro strips. Use a hot-glue gun to attach the strips to the balls. (The more balls you have, the better the game.)

Then declare a Velcro war among the kids. All combatants must wear a fluffy wool sweater to qualify them to carry weapons (the prepared plastic balls). They should also wear some kind of eye protection. In the church or at a school, identify a playing area that includes lots of hiding places accessible by more than one route.

The following rules will get you started. Once it's all-out war, make up the rules as you go along.

- Once a Velcro ball sticks, it's a wound. It can't be taken off. Three wounds equal a kill.
- Play the game as teams. The smaller the group, however, the better it is to play every man for himself.
- You may expand the target area by requiring all players to wear wool caps.
- The harder the throw, the less likely balls are to stick and the more likely they are to injure, so attack with lobs and crafty tosses.

Dik LaPine

Tarzan Kickball

Jazz up traditional kickball by setting up a portable sound system and playing background music of prerecorded bits of fast-moving, motion-picture soundtracks. You can also throw in some lively old stuff like "Oklahoma!" Your local library is a good resource for music. As you're making the tape, every once in a while dub in a Tarzan yell (also from the library). The cassette should run about 35 minutes, with 10 to 15 Tarzan yells interspersed throughout the recording.

With the music playing in the background, play regulation kickball, with the following addition: When players hear the Tarzan yell, they must immediately stop playing, no matter what the action is. The kicking team must run to their team base in center field and squat down, while the fielding team runs to their team base behind home plate and squats down.

Making the teams run through each other to get to their bases adds to the excitement of the game. The first team all together and squatting down receives 10 points.

Once the winner is determined for that yell, normal play resumes exactly where it left off. Runners return to their positions on the bases, and the ball is returned to whomever had it at the time of the yell. Runs are scored as usual. The team with the most runs at the end of the time period wins.

To play longer than 35 minutes, just rewind the tape. Assign a judge to say which team is first to be all together and squatting after the yell.

    For a variation let each team bat once through the lineup, then switch to outfield.

Rich Cooper and Tim Maughan

Puzzle Relay

You'll need five sponsors, a large gymnasium or field, and two new 25-piece children's jigsaw puzzles.

- Mark one box with an X, and mark the back of each piece from that puzzle with an X as well.
- Mark the other box with a Z, and mark each of the corresponding pieces with a Z.
- Mark 16 small envelopes with an X, place one piece from the X puzzle in each envelope, and seal it. Put the nine remaining pieces back in their box.
- Do likewise for the 16 pieces from the Z puzzle.
- Set up a big table at home base, then designate five checkpoints about 30 to 40 yards away from home.
- Of the 32 envelopes, give to each of four sponsors four X envelopes and four Z envelopes.
- To the fifth sponsor give the two puzzle boxes.
- Assign one sponsor to each checkpoint; the sponsor with the boxes goes to checkpoint five.

Now divide all the kids into an X team and a Z team. Choose a team captain for each team, then divide both teams into four equal subteams.

While the two team captains stay at home base, each subteam makes the round of the checkpoints in a different order:

> Group A: 1-2-3-4-5
> Group B: 4-1-2-3-5
> Group C: 3-4-1-2-5
> Group D: 2-3-4-1-5

The entire subteam must travel to and from each checkpoint together. The sponsor at each checkpoint gives each subteam a task to perform; upon completion of the task, the sponsor gives the group one envelope for their team's puzzle. Here are sample tasks:

> Checkpoint 1: Sing one verse of "Pharaoh Pharaoh."
> Checkpoint 2: Recite John 3:16 backward.
> Checkpoint 3: Sing "Deep and Wide" with hand motions while running in place.
> Checkpoint 4: Form a six-person pyramid and recite the Pledge of Allegiance.
> Checkpoint 5: (captain only) Do an impersonation of Elvis.

Each subgroup must return to home base after each checkpoint and hand the envelope to their captain. The captain will put the unopened envelopes on the table. When all the envelopes are in and the entire team—that is, all four subteams—has returned to home base, the team captain must then go to checkpoint five, complete the task given, and return to home base with the box containing the remaining pieces to the team's puzzle. The envelopes are then torn open and the puzzle is completed by the team. The first team to complete its puzzle wins. *Gary Tapley*

Swedish Baseball

This variation of baseball is most effective with 25 or more participants. Teams are divided equally with one team out in the field and the other at bat. No bats or balls are used. All you need is a Frisbee.

The batter comes to the plate and throws the Frisbee out into the field. The fielding team chases down the Frisbee and tries to return it to a garbage can that is next to home plate. The Frisbee must be tossed in rather than simply dropped in. Meanwhile, the batter runs about 10 feet to the first base, then to the second base about eight feet away and begins to circle them. Every lap is one point for the batting team, and the runner continues until the Frisbee is in the can. All the players on the batting team get to be up each inning. There

are no outs.

After two or three innings, the score can get quite high. You'll need to have a scorekeeper who can keep track of all the points. *David Rasmussen*

Ultimate Football

Guaranteed to tire the most rambunctious junior high boys, this game requires only a Frisbee and lets everyone play quarterback and receiver.

Play on a football-type field with goal lines at either end. The object is to cross the goal line with a Frisbee. Play consists not in running (yet), but in passing the Frisbee in order to move it downfield.

Here's the shift to football: If the Frisbee holder does not throw it by the time a covering opponent counts to 10, the Frisbee holder is free to run with the Frisbee—and also free to be tackled by the opposing team if he does not throw on the run to a teammate. The Frisbee changes teams in the case of a tackle, an interception, or an incomplete pass.

Needless to say, your junior high boys will get their fill of tackling and running with this game! *John Krienke*

2

Outdoor Games For Small Groups

Flexibility is the key here. While these games work best in groups of fewer than 30 people, you can tweak most of them to work for larger groups, too. And while some require a large playing area, many can be played in a small yard.

Pie Tin Toss

For this game, you will need to secure the use of six high hurdles, like those used at a track meet. If you can't get real ones, just improvise. Line the hurdles up as in a regular hurdle race.

Team members run with a pie tin filled with shaving cream. When they come to the hurdle, they must throw the pie tin into the air, go under the hurdle, catch the pie tin on the other side, and continue until they have gone under all six hurdles. That person then runs back and tags the next team member in line, who repeats the action.

Each team is timed, and the best time wins. If a runner drops a pie tin, she must go back to the beginning and try again.
Linda Thompson

Inland Surfing

Who needs a beach for a beach party? Your kids can surf your backyard turf with this board, made from an old ironing board reinforced with 2x4-foot crossbars that are grooved in order for the board to sit on ropes slung between trees (see diagram). Decorate the top of the surfboard with contact paper and automotive striping, supply a mattress or other cushioning for the inevitable wipeouts, then—watch out! Surf's up as two people shake the ropes to create waves and surfers try their best to ride them out. Run a timed competition—record contestants' best times or the average of several tries.
Jim Bell

notches in 2x4's to sit on ropes at intersection of ropes 1 & 2

old ironing board (view of bottom)

2x4 end view

Crazy Baseball

Create teams of five or more players. With a Nerf ball and bat, play like regular baseball. Here's the crazy part: After a hit, batters can run to any base—but they cannot run through the pitcher's circle. Base runners score not by touching home plate, but by touching all three bases—first, second, and third—though in any order. Teams get six outs.
David Killinger and Chris Moore

Tennis Ball Golf

Set up a golf course using boxes (big ones for amateurs, small ones for pros) in a park or some other large open area. Golfers toss a tennis ball, attempting to get it inside the box for each hole. Boxes should be numbered one through nine (or 18).

You can make this game as easy or as difficult as you want, depending on the location of the boxes, and how the ball is tossed. You can require that all tosses be underhand, or through the legs, over the shoulder, bounced, or however you wish. Usually a player will put the ball into the box only to watch it bounce out. *Dave Mahoney*

Pop-Can Bowl

Divide your group into two teams; position them on opposite halves of a recreation room, gymnasium, or other playing area; and supply players with several playground balls. Between the two teams is a three-foot-wide "can zone," where dozens of empty pop cans stand.

Players must bowl the balls into the cans in order to knock them into the other team's playing area, though without crossing into the "can zone" themselves. The team with the least cans in its area after two minutes of playing wins. *John Krueger*

Two-On-Two Basketball

Here's a twist to the standard two-on-two game that's especially adaptable to tournament play. Each two-person team designates one of its members as the stationary shooter (Player S), who must remain at one end of the free-throw line. Player S cannot move her feet, and only she can do the shooting for her team. The remaining person on each team is the moving player (Player M), who grabs, rebounds, blocks shots, intercepts passes—everything but shoot.

Variations are endless. In coed games designate the girls as shooters, the guys as moving players. Or place your shooters anywhere on the court in order to vary the difficulty of the shots. Or add players and designate more shooters or more moving players. *Andrew Winters*

Human Pinball

The more the merrier in this fast, fun, indoor or outdoor ball-tag game. Give a playground ball to a group of at least 10, then explain the following rules:

- The object is to be the last one standing. Players who are hit with the ball and fail to catch it must kneel. If someone catches a thrown ball, then the thrower must kneel.
- When players get the ball, they cannot run or walk with it—they must throw from where they obtained the ball.
- Though they cannot move around, kneelers can still play while on their knees. They can stand again if they touch a standing person or hit someone with the ball.

Thud Gudnason

Croquet Pool

Mark off a 30-by-20-foot area of smooth ground with rope—this is your pool table. For pockets, lay speed cones, small buckets, etc., on their sides at the corners and at the

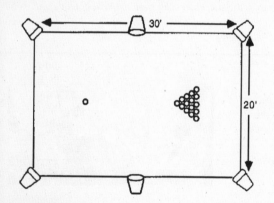

midpoint of the 30-foot sides, pool-table fashion. With enough croquet balls for your group (pool uses 15), designate one as the cue ball and begin the game by breaking the triangle.

From here, the game is played just like pool: the first one (or team) to sink his croquet balls into the cones wins. Mark the balls by color, stripe, etc. And don't forget to save the eight-ball for last!

Michael W. Capps

Score Ball

This variation of baseball is a great equalizer of talent—nonathletic types do as well as your group's jocks. All you need is an indoor or outdoor playing area marked into zones (see diagram), a bat, and three differently colored Nerf balls.

Divide into two teams. The fielding team spreads out in the "field" while the team at bat sends its first member to the plate to hit.

Here's how to play:

A batter gets only three pitches; three strikes put him out, as does a fly ball that a fielder catches.

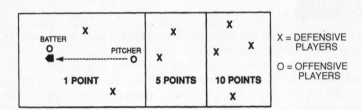

| BATTER
O ◄- - - - - - - - - - - - - - PITCHER
O | X

X | X

X | X

X | X = DEFENSIVE
PLAYERS |
| 1 POINT
X | 5 POINTS | 10 POINTS
X | | O = OFFENSIVE
PLAYERS |

The three colored balls are pitched in the same sequence for each batter. Here's why: The first pitch (say, the red ball) is worth one point if it's hit; the second (yellow), two points; the third (blue), three points. Colored balls make it easy to keep track of the points. So a batter may choose either to hit whatever ball comes his way or to wait for the second or third pitch for more points.

There's more—the point value of a hit ball is multiplied by the point value of the zone it lands in.

For example, if the batter hits the second pitch (two points) into the middle zone (five points), she earns 10 points for her team. A hit, therefore, can earn anywhere from one to 30 points.

Play as many innings as you like! *Roger Rome*

Power Croquet

For this croquet variation, the bigger and more rugged the yard (or lot or field) the better. Unlike its traditional, genteel cousin, Power Croquet is set up with as many obstacles as you can find—or fabricate. For example, set wickets—

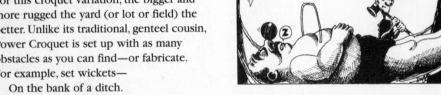

- On the bank of a ditch.
- Underneath a parked car.
- So that players must bank their balls off a cement block or a wall.
- So that players must navigate fallen branches.

In short, design a course similar in shape to normal croquet, but one full of obstacles to get over, under, around, or through. Put the ends of the course as far from each other as possible; if you're confined to a suburban lot, at least run the course around the house through both the front and back yards. *Dale Shackley*

Inner Tube Open

This equalizer can be won by sheer inexperience—so look out, golf pros! You'll need one or two nine-iron golf clubs; a dozen tennis balls (six yellow, six orange); a large blanket, quilt, or tarp; and a large, inflated inner tube.

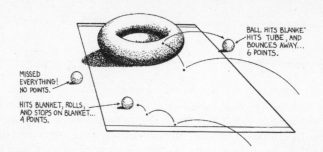

BALL HITS BLANKE
HITS TUBE, AND
BOUNCES AWAY...
6 POINTS.

MISSED
EVERYTHING!
NO POINTS.

HITS BLANKET, ROLLS,
AND STOPS ON BLANKET...
4 POINTS.

Mark a line 10 to 12 feet away from the front edge of the blanket; players take their strokes from behind this line. Place the inner tube on the far edge of the blanket.

Players get six strokes to earn points in the following ways:

Ball hits blanket	**1 point**
Ball stays on blanket	**3 points**
Ball hits inner tube	**5 points**
Ball stays inside inner tube	**20 points**

Points are awarded cumulatively. That is, if a ball hits the inner tube (5 points), rolls across the blanket a ways (1 point), and remains on the blanket (3 points), the player earns 9 points. Or if a ball hits the inner tube but bounces away without touching the blanket, that player earns 5 points. Whoever has the most points wins. Play by teams or individually.
Neil Zobel

Frisbee Swat

What you'll need for this active game are two (or more) Frisbees, two chairs, two cones (or water bottles), two teams, and a rolled-up newspaper for each player. At each end of the playing area, place a chair with a cone on its seat. The purpose is for each team to knock the other team's cone off the chair with a Frisbee. Points are awarded for each knockdown.

Team members pass the Frisbees to each other as they work their way down the field. No one is allowed to run with the Frisbee—they can only pass it. Team members hold a newspaper in one hand, which is used for knocking down the opponent's Frisbee, and use the other hand to catch and throw their team's Frisbee. To play the game teams must attempt to score on offense and at the same time maneuver around on defense to swat the opponent's Frisbee out of the air.
d Martinez

Ring Toss

This is just like the traditional carnival game—except that students are the bottles (perhaps with traffic cones on their heads) and Hula Hoops are the rings. Arrange the game to fit your group or your event. Have teams of two take turns tossing the hoops over each other, after each toss taking a step backward to increase the distance between them. Or have students step up to a line one at a time and face a group of bottles, and give each thrower three tries to ring a peer (the bottles further away from the throwing line are worth more points).
Michael Capps

Trac-Ball Tourney

Here are two games—an outdoor field game and an indoor gym game—that use Trac-Ball scoops—something like the Mexican jai alai. You can pick up a Wham-O Trac-Ball set (two scoops and a ball or two) from most department, toy, or sporting-goods stores.

   * Trac Football. Remember the variation of football called Speedball or Razzle Dazzle Touch Football—where the quarterback must pass, and then receivers themselves can pass anywhere on the field in order to move the ball toward the goal? Play with Trac-Ball scoops and a Trac-Ball ball—and you've got Trac Football. Only three rules:

1. Play is dead not by touching or tackling the ball carrier, but when the ball touches the ground. Defensive strategy, then, calls for interfering with a throw or a reception and trying to knock the ball from a carrier's scoop. A team gets four downs in which to score. (See rule 3 about first downs.)

2. The ball is advanced only by throwing it, not by running it. A player may scramble behind the line of scrimmage (the point at which the play begins, or the point at which a receiver catches the ball), but a ball carrier may not run beyond the line of scrimmage until he hurls the ball. Teammates (potential receivers) may run anywhere, of course.

3. Two complete passes earn a first down. Those passes may come within a single play, or one may occur in one down, the other during another down. Any time during the four downs that a team completes its second pass, it earns a first down. (If your group gets good at Trac Football, increase the difficulty of earning first downs: Require three completes for a first, award two consecutive first downs if a team completes three passes within a single play, etc.)

   Interceptions, kickoffs, hikes, punts—they're all done similarly to regular touch football, but within the limitations imposed by these three rules.

   Six scoops may be a minimum amount of equipment to start out with. Some Trac Football players don't think a maximum exists. "The more, the better!" they say.

* Macho Trac-Ball. This lacrosse-like game will become a favorite of the rough-and-tough guys in your group. Situate two equal teams of any size on opposite sides of a center line. Now supply indoor hockey nets at either end (or draw or tape an area on the two opposite baseline walls, or simply use the closed gym doors as goals if they are at the proper ends of the gym).

Equip players with two balls and at least six Trac-Ball scoops. The object of the contest is to hurl a ball into the opponent's goal—but at no time can players cross the center line into their opponents' side. Teams may defend their goals by putting as many of their players as they want in front of the goals. In so doing, they'll get stung a bit by balls flung at their goal, but they'll also be thwarting attempts on their goal by the opposition across the center line.

The twist to this dodging game is the spin that Trac-Ball scoops put on the ball. It's hard to judge curves coming at you 60 miles per hour. *Dik LaPine*

These games are geared toward groups of 30 or more and are designed to be played in a gymnasium, fellowship hall, or similar room. But no matter how large your group is or what the confines of your meeting area are, you'll find crowd breakers, mixers, and contests that will work for you.

Mix 'Em Up

This variation on musical chairs works best with at least 15 players—the more the merrier. Set up a circle of chairs, one for each player except the leader. All the players sit down.

The leader calls out a random characteristic present in the group—"Everyone with purple socks!" All players who share that characteristic get up and scramble for new seats vacated by other players doing the same thing. The leader also darts for a seat. When the seats are filled, one player is left standing—who chooses the next characteristic, and so on.

If absolutely nothing comes to mind, "It" can always say, "Mix 'em up!" at which all players get up and find new seats. *Christopher Graham*

Dot To Dot

Before this game, buy two packages (each package a different color) of one-half-inch self-sticking circle labels and number them one through half the number of kids in your group—this is, if there are 30 in your group, number one color of circles 1 through 15. Do the same for the other color circles. Bring along a few balls of kite string or embroidery yarn as well as some rolls of masking tape.

Divide the kids into two teams (or more, if your group is large), give each team a package of the numbered "dots," instruct all players to stick a dot on their foreheads—then have them mingle, perhaps playing another crowd breaker so that the members of the two or more teams are thoroughly mixed. At a signal all players should stand still, and a selected captain from each team is given the string and tape and told to string her team dot-to-dot fashion, in order according to the numbers stuck to her teammates' foreheads. Captains can tape the string where they want on their teammates, and the first team finished wins.

Can you guess the fitting reward? A children's dot-to-dot book! *Keith Curran*

Shuffle The Deck

Here's a simple, lively way to break a large group down into smaller ones—or to play just for fun. Distribute a deck of playing cards (or Rook cards) to the group, one per person. Then you call out different combinations, like these:

• "Get in a group that adds up to 58."
• "Find three people of the same suit."
• "Find five numbers in a row, of any suit."

- "Find your whole suit."
- "Find four of you—four 3s, four 8s, etc."

For larger groups use multiple decks of cards; for smaller groups eliminate cards. Then create your own combinations! *Scott Oas*

Nine-Legged Race

Just for fun or to demonstrate the value of working together, this variation of the three-legged race is best for large groups and lots of space.

Divide the kids into groups of eight or so (the numbers don't matter as long as the teams are even). Place five kids on one side of the playing field, and the team's remaining three kids opposite them across the field. From the five-kid side, two of them begin a traditional three-legged race. When they reach the other side, they add another team member, turn, and run back. At each end of their course, they tie up with another teammate until all eight kids are strung together at the ankles and running the last length. The first across the finish line wins. (The fun is watching them figure out how to turn around—but don't tell them this.)

For heightened hilarity, use thin plastic trash bag strips as ties, and add this rule—if a tie breaks, they have to stop and either re-tie it or replace it.

And even though you may not have specified the game as a foot race, the teammates cannot drop to their knees and pull themselves along with their hands. *Phillip Lopez*

Ring-Net Ball

Here's a basketball-type game for gym night. As in baseball, the defense scatters around the basketball court. From the sideline at midcourt, an offensive batter throws a basketball into the field. He then runs out to the circle at midcourt—the base—and runs around it as many times as possible before the defense can grab the ball and sink a basket. Score one point for each completed circle around the base. Everyone on the team throws before the inning switches. *Phil Blackwell*

Basketcase

Here are the crazy twists to this basketball variation: the ball is carried overhead instead of dribbled down the court, and it is passed to a teammate by rolling it. Baskets are scored by throwing the ball up through the bottom of the hoop. Here are some details players need to know:

- Teammates of the player who passes the ball may use their hands to pick it up and carry it downcourt.
- Opponents of a passer, however, cannot use their hands to intercept a passed (rolled) ball—they must snare the ball between their feet, after which they can use their hands to carry and pass the ball.
- Four shots are taken this way: the shooter rolls the ball to a teammate along the key, who

may pick it up and make a basket a la "Basketcase."
Play to 21—the odd points must come from a foul shot. *Michael W. Capps*

Fuzzyball

Here's a take-off on baseball perfect for indoors and for groups of 10 to 50. You'll need a fuzzyball—one of those softball-sized nursery toys with a rubber center and fabric (usually yarn) covering—and a plastic Wiffleball bat. (In a pinch you can use a Nerf ball and a broom.) Lay out home plate and three bases, divide players into two teams, and play ball—well, play fuzzyball.

Here are the differences:

- With a hit, players run first to what is normally third base, then to what is normally first base, then to what is normally second base, then home.

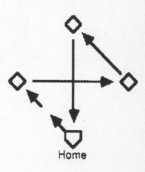

- Runners are put out only when tagged by hand or when tagged by the ball below the shoulders. Catching fly balls and tagging bases are not outs.
- Everyone on a team gets to bat once, and only once, each inning, regardless of how many outs. (Outs retire runners from base running; they don't determine the length of the inning.)
- The team at bat supplies its own pitcher. A maximum of three pitches are allowed to each batter. Two strikes constitute an out.

Ralph Gustafson

People Ball

Here's a basketball game that includes everyone, not just the competitive hoopsters. After you divide your group into two teams, five from each team should take their place on the court and play regulation basketball—except that they cannot dribble the ball. In fact, they cannot move when they have the ball.

Here's how the ball is moved down the floor: all the rest of the team not on the court spreads out along both sidelines, alternating teams. The 10 players on the court must throw the ball to a sidelines teammate, who then throws it to a court player on his team. There are plenty of chances for interception, of course, both on the sidelines and the court.

Players should wear identifying colors or jerseys for quick recognition. There are no fouls on sideliners, and the ball is always put into play by a sideliner. *Michael W. Capps*

Indoor Soccer

With a large, unfurnished room and a small (six-inch) soccer ball, you can stage your own indoor soccer tournaments. Adjust the rules to suit your own situation and to keep the game swift and safe. Divide large groups into teams of five—two teams play for two minutes, then are replaced by two new teams. Or keep 'em guessing with a tag-team variation—divide a big group into two teams, which divide themselves again into groups of five. At the whistle (blown at varying intervals) players stop playing where they are, run to their sideline, and tag a new group of teammates who resume play.

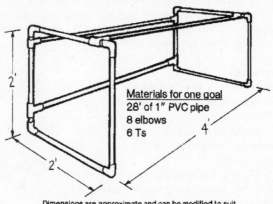

Materials for one goal
28' of 1" PVC pipe
8 elbows
6 Ts

Dimensions are approximate and can be modified to suit different situations.

You can construct your own goals with just a few lengths of PVC pipe and some inexpensive cargo netting (see diagram).

So that you can disassemble them easily for storage, don't glue the pipe.

Dimensions are approximate and can be modified to suit different situations. *Jim Reed*

Skizbomania

Here's a search-and-destroy game in the dark—squirt guns are the weapons, and the targets are pages or pieces of pages from paint-with-water coloring books attached to players' backs. After the battle, the defeated platoon is the one with most hits—and the hits will be obvious when the lights are turned on again.

You can make the game as elaborate or as simple as you want with these modifications:

- Play it in a pitch-dark room in any case. If some indication of players' whereabouts is wanted, each kid can wear a strip of glow-in-the-dark tape on a headband or pinned to his front or back. Or use a strobe light.
- If you want teams identifiable in the dark, arrange a few small glow-strips in a team pattern.
- For more accurate scoring, cut the coloring-book pages into quarter-sized circles; then glue, tape, or staple them onto a paper towel, which is pinned to the back or front of a player. Then again, players can simply wear whole or half pages of coloring books pinned to them, and scoring can be more general.

Although it's not necessary, it is convenient to have a refill place for the squirt guns in the same room. Each game could be longer, too. *Steve Sayer*

Arena Nerfketball

If you have a large room and can mount Nerf ball baskets and backboards at either end (or construct simple, portable frames to mount them on), your group can generate all the enthusiasm of a tournament play-off. Create two teams that must devise team names and cheers. Have groups of five rotate in and out every few minutes to give everyone a chance to play. Use refs to maintain order and keep the game moving. And since the baskets may be fragile, tape off the area four feet out from each basket and declare it out-of-bounds.

Other rules that keep the game active:
- Since Nerf balls can't be dribbled, players must pass after taking three steps.
- No touching opponents.
- No roughness.
- Play stops at ref's whistle, and ball goes to ref (violation of this rule results in a penalty).
- All penalties result in a free throw (free-throw shooters must rotate).
- Ref's decisions are final.

A fitting and frenetic finale? Invite everyone onto the floor for the game's last minute! *Jim Reed*

Parliff

This is a gym game for 16 or more kids, played with a basketball. One team spreads out across the court while the other goes up to "bat" next to one wall of the gym. The batter takes the ball and either punts or throws it in any direction (no boundaries). Immediately he or she then runs to the far wall, touches it, and runs back to touch the "home" wall. Meanwhile, the team in the "field" is chasing down the ball and passing it to a designated shooter under the goal next to their own home wall.

If the shooter can make the basket before the batter touches the home wall, the batter is out. If the batter makes it home first, his or her team wins a point for the "run." Allow three outs, and then the opposing team is up. Highest score after nine innings wins. *Chris Thompson*

Basket-Dodgeball

For this game you need a gym or a full basketball court with two hoops, four basketballs, and a playground ball.

Divide players into four teams. Each team lines up in a corner of the court in tallest-to-shortest order (see diagram below). Each player on the team is assigned a number—1 for the tallest, 2 for the next tallest, and so on. (To accommodate uneven teams, assign some players two numbers.)

Here's how to play. After you make sure all players are sitting, yell out a number—"Three!" The four 3s leap up, grab their basketballs, and dribble them to the basket at the opposite end of the gym. Only when a player makes a basket can he run back to his team without dribbling and set down the ball.

And here's where the dodgeball enters. The first player back from replacing his basketball runs to center court, picks up the dodgeball, and begins the dodgeball game. Whoever he hits is out (the ball must hit the person without first bouncing)—unless the intended victim catches the ball, in which case the thrower is out. Woe to the player who's still struggling with making a basket when the other three start dodgeball!

When three players are eliminated from a dodgeball game, the survivor's team earns one point. Return balls and players to starting positions, then call another number. Play as many rounds as you like, or play until a team reaches a predetermined score. With kids dribbling in the opposite directions and two of them shooting at the same basket, you'll get some wild collisions.

With few people or only one hoop, have just three teams that shoot in the same basket. Adapt the game for indoors with a Nerf ball. *Jeff Callen*

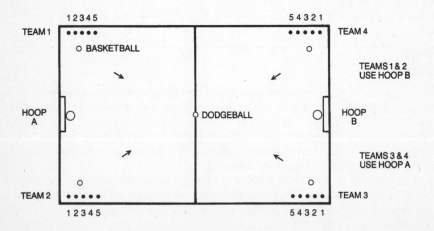

Switcher

Here's an indoors musical-chairs-type game ideal for retreats. Arrange the 36 chairs in a hexagon (or as few as 24), divide kids into six teams of six each, assign each team a number (one through six), and give the captain of each team a sign or large card with his or her team number on it. Have the players sit as teams, in numeric order, clockwise (see diagram).

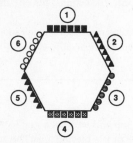 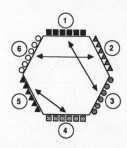

Now call out the first number pattern: "1-3, 2-6, 5-4—switch!" This means that, when you yell "switch!" teams one and three must exchange places, teams two and six must exchange places, and teams five and four must exchange places. (You should list lots of number patterns ahead of time and simply read them off during the game.) Each captain's sign should help get everybody to the proper section, but it's still mayhem.

Here's the competitive angle: the last person seated is out (the chair, however, is left in). If the captain is out, she gives the team-number sign to a teammate. Then you call out the next number pattern: "4-2, 1-5, 3-6—switch!" and so on, until only one player is left. An interesting variation is eliminating players down to the last person on each team only, then letting these few play the final rounds. *Michael W. Capps*

Head Hacky Sack

Give each team (seven to 10 people per team) a punch-ball-type balloon. The teams form circles and try to keep the punch ball in the air using only their heads. Play by the same rules as hacky sack, except that the head is the only part of the body with which players can legally hit the ball. If the punch ball falls to the floor, pick it up and start over. The team with the most consecutive hits is the winner. *Michael Frisbie*

Tapeworms

Set up a table at each end of the playing area, form a semicircular safety zone in front of each table with pylons or chairs (see diagram), and stick a bunch of two-inch-long pieces of masking tape to the front edge of each table (two pieces per team member).

The game starts as both teams pile into their own safety zones, grab one piece of tape each, and then enter the battle zone in order to stick the tape on their opponents' bodies, below the shoulders. Players can't remove the tape once they're stuck. After sticking

someone, players can return to their safety zone (for only 10 seconds) for one more piece of tape.

After a specified period of time, the game ends, teams count how many hits they've received, and the team with the least hits wins. Colored tape gives the game a brighter aspect, perhaps to designate teams. *Daniel Atwood*

Bail-o-Wack

This game is like volleyball, but it's played with a balloon and without a net. To set up use masking tape to make a straight line across the middle of the playing area. The length of the line in feet should be twice the total number of players on both teams (for example, for 10 players use a 20-foot line).

Divide into two teams, and have each team stand facing the other across the line (as if it were the net) in a single row on each side. Players should stand four feet apart from teammates, and two feet back from the line. Players cannot move from this position during play, though one foot may leave the floor to kick the balloon if the other stays in place.

center for Team A ↓

TEAM A	X	X	X	(X)	X	X	X
TEAM B	0	0	0	(0)	0	0	0

center for Team B ↑

The object is to volley a balloon back and forth across the line without allowing it to touch the floor on your team's side. The balloon can be batted with hands or kicked. As with the ball in volleyball, contact with the balloon may alternate between players on the same team, but the balloon cannot be touched by the same player twice in a row. Unlike volleyball, however, teams are not limited to three contacts in order to get the balloon back over the line to the other team.

The middle player in each team's line is the "center." Each round begins with one of the centers serving by tapping the balloon across the line to the other team. The team that won the point in the previous round gets to serve. A team scores a point when the balloon touches the floor on the opposite team's side of the line. There is no out-of-bounds play, so if the balloon is batted over the heads of players and out of their reach, the opposite team scores a point. A team also scores a point when a player on the opposite team makes contact with the balloon twice in a row or moves out of position.

You'll need extra balloons in case one bursts and a referee to make sure players stay in position. *Phil Blackwell*

Wall Hockey

This is an indoor game that can be played by groups as small as six or as large as 50.

The playing area should be bounded on two sides by walls, where the players must line up in two equal teams, one team along each wall (see diagram).

At the other two ends of the play area goals are set up, using street hockey nets, boxes, or chairs. The object of the game is to score the most goals by hitting the puck or ball into the opponent's net.

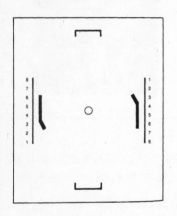

Players must count off in order, numbering themselves in one direction on one team and in the opposite direction on the other team. Each team is given a hockey stick (a broom will do if you use a larger ball).

To begin play, all players must place one hand on the wall behind them, and keep it there at all times during the game. Players on each team next gather to place their free hand on the hockey stick. Once everyone is holding the stick, the leader calls out a number, and the player from each team with that number takes his hand off the wall, grabs the stick, and goes out to face the opponent. The rest of the team members release the stock but must keep a hand on the wall. Failure to do so costs a player's team one point.

To make the game more interesting, call out other numbers during a play. The two players in the center must then drop their sticks where they are, return to their lines, and put a hand on the wall before the next player can go out. This also helps keep more kids in the game. With large groups of 50 or more, you may want to divide up into four teams—one pair with letters and one with numbers—and then call out numbers and letters alternately. *Brian Fullerton*

Balloon Bomb

Remember the leftover party balloon that you'd bounce around in the air when you were a child, trying to keep it from hitting the ground? What was rainy day entertainment then still works with youth groups today.

Formalize the game a bit—form two teams that try to hit the balloon away from the opposition, require that teams alternate hits (only one hit per team), and forbid hitting the balloon directly at the floor. Scoring can run like this: Intentional grounding scores a point

for the opposition, as does two consecutive hits by members of the same team. If the balloon touches the ground, the point goes to the opposition of the team that hit it last.

Variation: Instead of the two teams intermingling in the playing area, put them on opposite sides of a six-foot-wide dead zone, and permit—volleyball fashion—two hits per team (by different players) before returning the balloon across the dead zone. More than two hits per team or more than one hit per person scores a point for the opposition. If the balloon lands in the dead zone, the point is scored against the team that last hit it. A team serves until it loses a point.

* Balloon Bomb Dress-up Relay. For this variation of Balloon Bomb, each team needs a dress-up box with the same number and kinds of objects—old coat, gloves, hat, scarf, boots, etc. As teammates take their turns racing to the box and then dressing and undressing with the old clothes, they must keep a balloon in the air. If the balloon touches the ground, they must start their dressing over again. *Julie D. Anderson, Karen Friday, and Len and Sheryl DiCicco*

Teddy Bear Football

Although this game sounds corny, a little hype and the right mix of humor makes this flag-football perversion more than bearable. In fact, it's actually become an annual event at one church, drawing players and spectators alike.

It's traditional flag football, though played in a gym or fellowship hall—and with a teddy bear instead of a football.

In a gym roomy enough for running, passing, and—yes—kicking a teddy bear, erect goal posts from two-by-fours, or use crepe paper taped to the walls for field-goal markers. In a short gym, for instance, allow only five downs. If the team does not score, it must punt the bear to the other team or try for a field goal on the fifth down. (Be sure to use traditional punting and kicking formations.) You may want to include a girls-only quarter, followed by a boys-only quarter. During the remaining quarters, keep the girls active by requiring that a girl touch the ball once during each possession. In coed teams, of course, limit the physical

contact involved in blocking or running over people.

A 15-inch bear is just the right size; it will work well for kickoffs, passes, punts, and field goals. (The smaller stuffed bears just don't provide the same level of sadistic pleasure.) KIPP Brothers sells reasonably priced carnival bears (800/428-1153 or 317/634-5507). You may be able to borrow a bear, but the likelihood of returning it the way you received it is slim. In fact, you'll probably need a replacement bear to finish off the game—so get two.

Cue the referee to use creative calls like "Roughing the teddy!" Then play traditional flag football, modifying the rules to fit your situation.

Half-time? Offer a refreshment stand (free snacks,), a kazoo marching band, and the crowning of a queen (a guy dressed up like a girl). *Steve Smoker*

Turns And Trades

Form two concentric circles of equal numbers of kids facing each other. Tell the kids to trade one thing they have on for one thing the person facing them has on—jewelry, shoes, socks, belts, hats, etc. The players must then put on the items they traded for.

Now ask the inner circle to move three people to their right so that each player has a new partner. Partners must make another trade; but they cannot trade anything they've received in a trade. Next ask the outer circle to move two people to their right and repeat the trading process. Call for one more turn and trade.

Kids will now have run out of jewelry, shoes, etc., and may be getting embarrassed about another impending trade. So have some fun with them: tell the outer circle to move two people to the right again. You'll hear moans, but when they move, tell them to trade something that has already been traded. Repeat this twice.

Now tell them they have two minutes to retrieve all of their items. Offer a prize to the first one to bring all of the items up to you, or you can time the group to see how quickly they can all retrieve their things and then sit down. *Terry Linhart*

Group Juggle

This circle game is something like hot potato, with a dash of Concentration. Throw a ball to one person in a standing circle of kids. That person throws it to another, and so on until everyone has received and thrown the ball once—but exactly once. No one should get the ball a second time, which means each player needs to remember where the ball's been. If your group's frustration threshold is high, increase the speed of the game and add more balls. *Tom Jackson*

Balloon Bump

Here's an indoor game for moderately sized groups (20 or more kids). Divide players into groups of four to six or so; place about as many chairs as there are groups randomly around the room; place lots of deflated balloons on each chair; then instruct each group to form a huddle of people, arms around shoulders, in the middle of the room.

On "Go!" each huddle shuffles to a chair. One person from each huddle grabs a balloon, blows it up, ties it off, and drops it into the middle of the huddle. Players in the huddle must keep the balloon from touching the floor by pressing against the balloon with their stomachs. As they do so, they must move toward another chair to repeat the process. At the

second chair they visit, they must blow up two balloons; at the third chair, three balloons, etc.—all the while maintaining their huddle and keeping their balloons from falling to the floor.

If a balloon falls, the huddle must stop and put it back in the middle again (which takes time). A huddle cannot visit a chair where there is already another huddle working. Call time at three minutes, count how many balloons each huddle has in its middle, announce a winner—and play again! *Michael Capps*

Triangle Tag

Have kids gather into groups of four. Three of them should form a triangle by holding hands or wrists. The fourth person stands in the middle of the triangle.

Choose one group to be "It." A successful tag occurs only when the person in the middle of a triangle tags another middler. The trick, of course, is for the triangle to track with their middler, to anticipate his or her direction and strategy—or at least to hear the middler's verbal instructions. The other groups, of course, try to avoid being tagged while staying inside the boundaries.

Every few games rotate members within their group, so everyone gets a turn inside the triangle. (Besides being fun Triangle Tag can effectively introduce sessions about submission, humility, and cooperation.) *Alan Rathbun*

Off The Wall

Here's a high-energy competition that blends dodgeball with Capture the Flag.

Create a playing court in your gym (or large room, provided the walls are very sturdy) by assigning each wall a color and taping 50 inflated balloons of that color to the wall. Create a territory for each color that extends out 20 feet from the wall, leaving a large "free zone" in the center of the gym (see diagram). In the center of each of the four territories, set a "safe" (a large box). At the edge of each territory, mark off an area to be the team's "jail."

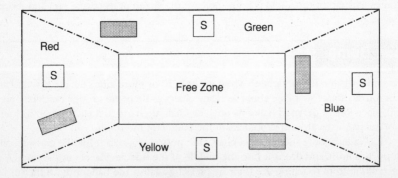

Now divide your group into teams—one team for each territory. Each team designates certain players as Invaders, Defenders, and one Jailkeeper.

- Invaders. Invaders try to hit opposing teams' balloons off the wall with soccer balls or playground balls thrown only from the central free zone. An Invader cannot throw a ball unless he or she remains in the free zone. Invaders may also steal balloons from an enemy's wall by invading their territory. Stolen balloons are taken back to the Invader's own team's safe. Invaders may not, however, steal balloons from an opponent's "safe."
- Defenders. Defenders defend their wall by catching or deflecting balls. They may capture Invaders by tagging them within the Defender's territory. Captured Invaders are taken to the jail. Defenders may not return balloons to the wall that were hit off.
- Jail rules. A team may ransom its Invaders who are in jail by exchanging three balloons from its safe for its incarcerated Invader. The team holding the Invader in jail may then return these recovered balloons to its wall.

Assign a time limit for the game to be played out. At the end of the game, each team earns five points for every balloon remaining on its wall and 10 points for every captured balloon still in its safe. *James Bell*

Indoor Games For Small Groups

These games will work best in groups of 30 or less; however, most of them can be adapted for use in larger groups. And while some require a large indoor space, such as a fellowship hall or gymnasium, others can be played in a living room.

Ping Bag

Several early-bird students in a youth group came up with this idea for passing time while waiting for slower groups to finish a discussion question. Every player has a Ping-Pong paddle to toss and catch a small bean bag. You can toss the bag to anyone in the circle—it's every man for himself. If players miss the bean bag, they're out. If the toss is determined by group consensus to be uncatchable, the tosser is out. The trick is to toss the bag so that it's difficult but still possible to catch by an aggressive player. When only one player is left in the circle, everyone rejoins the circle and round two begins. *Doug Partin*

Banana Duel

Team up your kids in pairs, have partners clasp their left hands, then tie those hands together. Give each player a banana with these instructions: they are to peel the banana any way they can (usually with teeth and right hands) before cramming it into their partner's mouth.

If your playing area can take the inevitable mess, enliven the game by blindfolding some or all the players. *Garr Williams, Jr.*

Kool-Aid Taste-Off

Ask three volunteers to sit in chairs facing the rest of the group. On a signal they each open a different flavored packet of Kool-Aid. Volunteers then lick just one finger and dip it into the packet. The person who in that manner can eat all of the Kool-Aid in the packet first wins. It's hilarious because they do not anticipate it being so sour, and they usually end up with it all over their lips. *Amy Zuberbuhler*

Pop Fly! Ground Ball!

The object of this indoor game for 25 or so players is to be the first of four teams to successfully throw or roll a colored Nerf ball among all its members and then back to the captain.

First arrange the chairs in a square, divide the group into four equal teams, and instruct members of each team to sit opposite their teammates—see the diagram on next page.

Next, give each team a different-colored Nerf ball. Volunteer one person on each team as captain; captains should sit at one of the ends of their team, and the four captains should sit at the same positions relative to their teams.

Here's how the game is played. Each captain tosses the team's Nerf ball across the square to a teammate opposite him. That player then tosses the ball back across the square to the player seated next to the captain—and so on.

You can imagine the delightful chaos of four teams of teenagers all trying to pass Nerf balls through the same confined area. The last person on the team to receive the ball tosses it back to the captain, after which everyone on that team stands up and yells—thus letting everyone else know they've finished.

Now here's what makes it fun: At any time the youth leader can yell "Ground ball!" At this signal all teams must immediately begin rolling their balls across the floor instead of throwing them. And when they hear "Pop fly!" they return to tossing the balls. It is legal for the leader to yell the same signal several times in succession—just to keep the kids guessing! *Michael W. Capps*

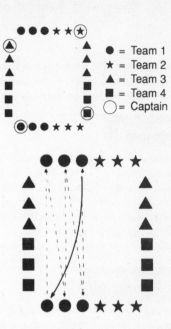

● = Team 1
★ = Team 2
▲ = Team 3
■ = Team 4
○ = Captain

Assault

Adapt the assault game of TV's "American Gladiators" to your church hall or youth room. Set up the playing area with four barriers, such as tables and desks, for runners to hide behind. Set aside a small area for the gladiators to stay in, and designate a finish area. Provide 50 or more tennis balls for the gladiators to use. Supply safety gear—goggles, head gear, knee pads, etc.—for runners to use while running the course.

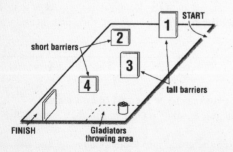

short barriers
tall barriers
START
FINISH
Gladiators throwing area

Give each runner one minute to run the course: from the start area to each of the barriers, trying to finish the course as quickly as possible—despite the barrage of tennis balls thrown by a pair of gladiators. Runners hit by a tennis ball are out.

Heighten the competition by placing an eight-foot-high target on the wall behind the gladiators. Then place a tennis ball behind each barrier. A runner successfully reaching a barrier may throw the tennis ball there. Players who hit the target win the round.

Record the times of those who finish the course, and reward the fastest times with an American Gladiator T-shirt or similar prize. *Bruce Smith*

Shooting Gallery

Blindfold three or four adult leaders and give them kazoos, party noisemakers, or something similar. They are the "ducks" in this shooting gallery, moving back and forth and bobbing up and down behind a wall or board that's five feet high or so, making "duck" noises all the while.

From about 10 feet away, kids have five throws of a beach ball at the "ducks." Most hits wins; carnival-type prizes are appropriate. *John Krueger*

Carnival Concentration

For this variation of the old TV game show "Concentration," ask one of the kids with artistic flair to create a Concentration-style puzzle to put on a bulletin board. The puzzle could be a common expression, a line from a popular song, the title from a TV show or movie, or a verse of Scripture. Then tape inflated balloons over the entire puzzle using clear tape.

When it's time to play, break the group into two or three teams. Teams take turns throwing darts at the balloons. When a player pops a balloon, that player's team gets 15 seconds to try to solve the puzzle. A team can only guess the puzzle when one of its members has popped a balloon. The winning team is the first to solve the puzzle successfully. *Jim Bell*

Q-Tip War

Divide your kids into two teams, separate them by a line down the middle of the room, give each team five or 10 Q-Tips per person and each person a straw—and open fire! The object for them is to blow-gun as many Q-Tips across the line onto the enemy's side of the room as possible before time runs out. Students can reload with Q-Tips shot over onto their side.

After the shooting ends, objective volunteers count the Q-Tips on each side, and the team with the lesser number wins. *Todd Ladd*

Office Chair Dodgeball

Junior highers love this. A person sits on a revolving, rolling office chair in the center of a circle of players, who throw a ball at the chair. The sitter, meanwhile, attempts to block shots against her chair. Whoever hits the chair with the ball becomes the new sitter.

With a little practice, a sitter becomes pretty good at spinning, rolling, and twisting as she dodges the ball. The back of the chair, on the other hand, makes a great target for throwers. *Steve Smoker*

Hovercraft Drag Races

Set out 8X11-inch sheets of paper and crayons, pencils, or markers. Instruct your students to design their own sports car—a flat, two-dimensional dream machine, colored from a bird's-eye view. Encourage them to use their imaginations—to name their cars, cover them with "sponsor" names and logos, and number them. Remind them to distinguish the front from the rear.

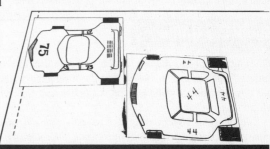

The drag strip is a table; provide start and finish lines. Owners of the hovercraft dragsters puff lightly on the rear of the vehicles to "float" them down the strip and across the finish line. Leaving the strip (falling off the table) and spin-outs (when the rear of the dragster is farther down the strip than its front) disqualify the "drivers," who can race the clock or each other in time trials and tournaments.

The final race can be a "Hovercraft 500." Set a square racetrack with four tables, divide your kids into teams, place some puffers on the inside of the track, then have each team race the clock and try to best each other's times. *Brett C. Wilson*

Popsicle-Stick Frisbee

The more players, the better for this game—plus you'll need lots of Popsicle sticks (for just 20 players, you'll need a total of 240 sticks). Mark off a fairly large room or a gym similar to a soccer field (see illustration)—two halves separated by a center line and a goal at each end (a goal should comprise about a quarter of a team's half of the floor).

Give every player a dozen Popsicle sticks, then divide them into two teams. When the clock starts—

- The offensive object is for each player to quickly assemble a pair of Popsicle-stick Frisbees, then try to land as many as possible in their opponents' goal.
- The defensive object is to block Popsicle-stick Frisbees from entering their goal.

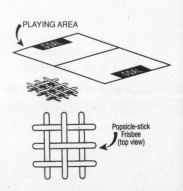

PLAYING AREA

GOAL

GOAL

Popsicle-stick
Frisbee
(top view)

Rules:

- Players may block flying (or sliding) Popsicle-stick Frisbees any way they wish with their bodies.
- Broken sticks should be removed from the game.
- Players cannot cross the center line or enter their goals.
- Popsicle-stick Frisbees in the goals must stay; but Popsicle-stick Frisbees that land in the

playing area may be used again.
- A team may want to designate some players offense, some defense, and some Frisbee builders—or all players can play all positions.

The game continues for a predetermined duration of time, or until all Popsicle-stick Frisbees have landed in a goal. *Len Cuthbert*

Balloon Mini-Golf

Here's another good variation of golf that you can set up in your church.

Provide the kids with plastic floor hockey sticks. These are the golf clubs. The golf balls are small, round balloons (about 4" in diameter). The holes are boxes and containers of various sizes.

Just number all the boxes and containers, and lay out your golf course all over the church—in and out of rooms, down hallways, up stairs, over water hazards (the baptistry), and so on. You might even set up some adverse weather conditions, like placing a fan along one of the fairways. Have someone preshoot the course to establish par for each hole. Since balloons are a bit tough to control, the game can become rather unpredictable, but that adds to the fun. *Wayne Mathias and Mark Boughan*

Go Fly A Kite!

For a March fling any time of year, bring a window fan and some yarn, and ask the kids to bring materials to make kites—paper, straws, Popsicle sticks, glue, Scotch tape. Announce a kite-flying contest, but tell everyone to bring what they need to make a kite. (Don't let them bring already-made kites.) The ones the group will fly must be several times smaller than regular kites because they'll be flown with the help of the yarn and the window fan.

Give the kids a set time to create small kites, using whatever materials they wish, just so long as the kite can stay up whenever the fan is blown at full blast (see diagram).

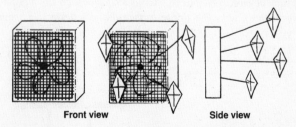

Front view   **Side view**

The best kites are those made in the traditional diamond shape. After everyone has made a kite, begin tying them to the fan one at a time with about three to four feet of yarn (shorter lengths if the yarn is heavy), and turn the fan on full blast, facing away from the house or into the center of the room. Add more kites and see how many you can fly without tangling them up together. This activity works well with a small youth group or study group. *Michael Capps*

Oddball Crawl

Begin this relay by creating two or more teams of eight to 10 players wearing their grubbies. At one end of a long room, line the teams up alternating boy-girl-boy-girl on each team. In each line players get on their hands and knees side by side on the floor. At the signal, the players at the end of each team's line closest to the wall begin crawling over and under their teammates as fast as possible. The stationary players alternately drop to the floor or arch up their backs (still keeping hands and feet on the floor) to make passage quicker for their traveling team member.

As soon as possible after the first players have crossed the second players, the second players may begin their trip over and under the stationary teammates. When traveling players reach the end of the line, they either lie flat or rise up to allow other players to pass over or under them. The relay continues until everyone on the team has successfully crawled over and under the rest of the team. The team that completes the relay first is the winner.

If your group is too small for two teams, form one team and play several rounds to go for the fastest team time. Have a camera handy to catch some of the action.

Awkward personal contact is rare, for the youths are sufficiently caught up in the race that they don't take time for mischief. *Michael W. Capps*

Fill My Cup

For this carnival or lock-in game, you'll need a table, a squirt gun, a small cup (an individual communion cup works fine), and a flat, dense surface that can deflect a stream of water from a squirt gun.

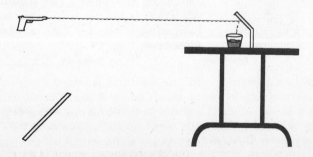

Anchor the small cup to the table with tape, arrange the deflector behind and above the cup (see diagram), and mark a line behind which shooters must stand. Time the shooters; the winner is the one to fill the cup to the line in the least time. Or set up two targets, and have shooters race each other. *Brett Wilson*

Toilet Bowl

Sequel to the cereal bowl and the Super Bowl, Toilet Bowl requires minimal set-up. Construct one or two toilet seat-and-lid combinations from heavy cardboard (better yet, use real toilet seats), prop them open so that the open lids serve as backboards, distribute a scotch-taped roll of toilet paper (the football) to each team, and make up some simple rules. The object of the game is to toss the toilet-paper football into the toilet.

Or make it a basketball free-throw game in tournament fashion, letting teams chart their advance to the Final Four and beyond. *E. Parke Brown*

Dressing In The Dark

To play this game you need piles of activity-specific clothing and blindfolds. Each pile must contain the same type of clothing. On 3x5-inch index cards write instructions for which activity players are to dress for, followed by a list of specific clothing to put on. For example, the card reads, "You are going to play tennis. Put on: sweatshirt, socks, tennis shoes, T-shirt." Another card might read, "You are going skiing. Put on: ski jacket, gloves, socks, overalls."

Divide your group into teams of seven or eight, and give the index cards describing the first outfit to one player from each team. After the players have memorized the clothing they are to put on, blindfold them and guide them to their team's pile of clothing. The blindfolded players have three minutes to pull from the pile the correct articles of clothing and dress themselves correctly and neatly—buttons in the correct buttonholes, shirts on inside in, and pants on correctly. The only help the blindfolded players have is their sense of touch and shouted clues from their teammates. At the end of three minutes, if no one is completely dressed, the leader decides who is the best dressed. Otherwise, the team whose player finished correctly dressing first gets the point. *Fay Wong*

Musical Sponge

This game is like musical chairs, but with a few changes. Use the same number of chairs as there are players. As the players circle the chairs, they hold onto the shoulders of the person in front of them. They are all blindfolded.

Before the music stops, the leader places a wet sponge on one of the chairs. The

unfortunate player who sits on the wet sponge when the music stops (or when the whistle blows) is out. *David Rasmussen*

Hidden In Plain Sight

In a relatively cluttered room, hide about 20 small items where they can be seen without having to open drawers or move other items. A shoelace can be wrapped around a chair leg, a dollar bill can be folded up and wrapped around a book spine, a pen can be placed atop a door frame with only the end showing, a button can be taped to a doorknob. Write out and photocopy a list of the things you've hidden—a pen, a bobby pin, a clothespin, a match—and then place a duplicate of each hidden item on a tray beside the lists.

When the kids are ready to play, give them each a copy of the list of hidden items, and leave the tray of duplicate items out for comparison. Set a time limit for the players to search the room to find each of the listed items. They are not to remove the items; they are only to note the location of each item. The winner is the player who finds the most items within the time limit. *Lyn Wargny*

Tic-Tac-Dart

On a large bulletin board, stick strips of masking tape in order to form a big tic-tac-toe figure with 18-inch squares. Tape three or four inflated balloons inside each of the nine squares.

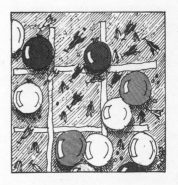

Divide your group into two teams. A player from the first team throws a single dart, trying to pop a balloon. If she succeeds, the next in line from her team attempts to pop another; if she fails, the other team sends a thrower to the line to try. The catch is this: Whichever team pops the last balloon in a square claims that square with an X or O.

You don't need darts, either—lay out the tic-tac-toe design and balloons on the floor, and drop sharpened pencils on them to pop them. *Michael W. Capps*

Frisbee Bowling

A number of people can play this game, and very little skill is required. To set up, all you need is a table, 10 paper cups, and three Frisbees or other flying discs. The cups are stacked in a pyramid several inches away from the far edge of the table. From a distance of about 20 feet, each player gets three attempts to knock as many of the cups as possible onto the floor, by hitting them with the Frisbee.

Each cup is worth one point. You can call each round a frame as in regular bowling, with a game consisting of as many frames as you like. If more than five people are playing,

keep a pencil and paper handy to keep track of the score. To keep the game moving, players can take turns throwing the Frisbees, retrieving them, and restacking the paper cups.
Deborah Cusson and Sean Mahar

Spell My Feet

The object of this hilarious game is for players to form words as quickly as they can. Two teams of five members each sit facing the audience. Using a large black marker, the leaders inscribe letters on the soles of the feet of the players.

The first player on each team gets an A on one foot and an N on the other; the second receives an E and a T; the third G and R; the fourth O and M; the fifth S and P.

The leader then calls out a word, and the group that is able to line up their feet to spell that word in the shortest amount of time wins that particular round.

- Easy word, worth five points each: MASTER, ROAST, SMEAR, TOGS, SNORE
- More difficult phrases, worth 10 points each: TEN PROMS, GET SPAM, GREAT SON, MORE NAPS
- The last series, worth 20 points per word, requires teams to compose their own words: the team using the most letters to form a word or combination of words wins the round.

Jim Johnson

Balloon Pong

All set up for table tennis, only to find no Ping-Pong balls? Get some balloons and play this slo-mo version of Ping-Pong.

Line your kids up in two lines, one against each end of the Ping-Pong table. Players play according to regular Ping-Pong rules—except that they hit a balloon instead of a ball (weighted with a marble inside, if necessary) and play with a single paddle. After a player hits the balloon, he slides the paddle across the table under the net to the player opposite him, who grabs the paddle before the balloon arrives and returns the balloon, Ping-Pong fashion. When a player makes his shot and slides the paddle to the other player, he scoots out of the way to the back of his line as quickly as possible.

Slower players may bend the rules a bit and keep the balloon aloft with their breath if they need time to snatch the paddle.

- Wacky Balloon Pong. Place a ball of Silly Putty inside a seven-inch balloon and partially blow up the balloon. Clip the knot off as close as possible and you've got a durable balloon that moves in swirls. *David Washburn and Doug Partin*

Team Nintendo

Borrow or rent a big-screen TV and the latest Nintendo offering (or other computer game popular among your students) for two teams of kids to battle for the video-game championship.

Start the game with one person from each team at the controls and the rest of the team standing 10 feet behind the players. Players have 30 seconds at the controls—you manage the stopwatch—while their teams cheer them on. After 30 seconds the next two players run up to the controls and take over, hopefully without missing a shot. When all members of the teams have taken their turn playing, round one is over and the score is recorded.

Play as long as enthusiasm lasts and promise a stupendous prize to the team with the most points. *Jeff Koch*

Strobe Ball

Try playing the old familiar volleyball or four-square in a room lit only by a strobe light (available at electronics shops). It's surprising how difficult it becomes to keep a semblance of coordination. Kids will be swinging at balls and usually missing. *Bill Aldridge*

Marshmallow Wall Golf

Take your kids on a trip to your homemade driving range. Find a room with a high ceiling and try this low-budget thriller.

The advance preparation is simple. Hang on a wall a large piece of butcher paper that goes from ceiling to floor. Draw a series of greens and a water hazard, each with designated points (see diagram).

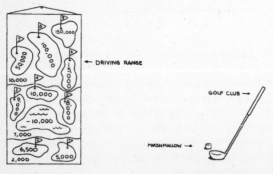

Try to hit a marshmallow onto one of the greens with a golf club; if you succeed, you get the number of points marked on the green. If you hit a spot outside of the green, you get the number of points marked in that particular area. If you hit the water hazard, you lose 10,000 points. The person with the highest number of points wins. *Doug Newhouse, Brian Cheek, and Michael Frisbie*

Dip And Stick

Create several girl-guy pairs. Each girl is given a pack of Lifesavers—the fruit-flavored ones, not the minty ones. On "Go!" each girl rips open her pack, then dips the Lifesavers in a glass of water and sticks them to her partner's face. If one falls off, she can pick it up and dip it and stick it on again. First pair to have the entire pack sticking to the guy's face wins. Or give teams a time limit; then if more than one pair gets their entire packs on the guys' faces, judge the winner by how long beyond the time limit the Lifesavers stay stuck to a face.

For ultimate stickiness, girls should put all the Lifesavers in the water at once, then pull them out to stick them on their partners' faces. *Steve Bridges and Rodney Oxford*

Masking-Tape Maze

If you have a fairly large room with a clean floor, a few rolls of masking tape will set you up for this tag game. It requires your kids to pretend that the wide tape strips that you lay down on the floor, maze fashion, represent invisible though impenetrable walls that cannot be crossed, jumped, or reached through. You'll probably want some refs to watch for corner-cutters and wall-climbers, who can be penalized by being made "It."

An autumn variation: play outside with raked-up lines of leaves instead of tape.

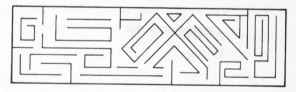

States

Everyone sits in a circle and takes the name of a state (Tennessee, Oregon, etc.). One person chosen to begin the game stands in the middle of the circle with a rolled-up newspaper (not too thick). When the newspaper-wielder calls out the name of a state, the person who represents that state must stand up and call out the name of another state before the newspaper-wielder can whack him (below the neck) with the newspaper. The round continues until the whacker in the center actually whacks a state-person below the neck before the latter calls out another state. The whackee then becomes the whacker and accordingly takes his or her place in the center, rolled newspaper in hand.

Just a few guidelines:

- You must call the name of a state that's represented in the group.
- You cannot call the state that just called you.
- You cannot call the state of the person in the middle.

Action can get fast and furious between just a few states, so occasionally redistribute the states among the players so that everyone participates. *Lynn H. Pryor*

Turnover

Form two teams of four or more players each. Using a volleyball and regulation net and court, play volleyball, but with this difference: The player whose mistake gives the other team the serve or a point will be turned over to play on the opposing team's side.

It gets heroic as one team dwindles to two or even one player who must stand 10 or 11 opponents. *Greg Miller*

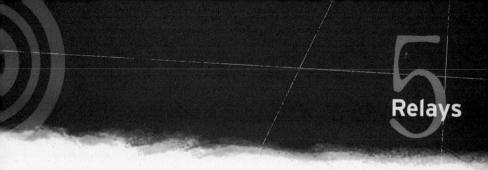

Nothing fosters a sense of teamwork, camaraderie, and often pandemonium quite like a good old relay race. Relays require team members to perform a given task, one teammate after another, as quickly as possible. Relays call for teams of equal numbers and can be run indoors or outdoors with nearly any size group.

The Dough-Tongue Shuffle

This is a relay game in which the young people are divided into two equal groups. Each group lines up, with players one behind the other. Then the first person in each line is given a large donut (preferably plain). On a signal, the first person in each group must run up to and round a given obstacle while holding the donut by sticking his tongue through its hole—no hands allowed. (This usually requires that the head be tilted back and the tongue pointed upward.)

After running around the obstacle, he must go to a designated area where a judge is waiting. Then each runner must eat his donut (to the satisfaction of the judge) and receives another donut from the judge (in his hand). The runner then carries this second donut to the next person in the relay line. The first runner places the donut in position on the next runner's tongue, and the relay continues. The first team to complete the relay by running all its members shouts "THE DOUGH-TONGUE SHUFFLE!" and wins.
Joe Harvey

Whisper The Flavor Relay

Using assorted flavors of Lifesavers or other hard candy or jelly beans, play this relay in which team members guess the flavor of the candy they are tasting.

Divide the group into teams of five to eight players. Each team chooses one member to be the distributor, to whom you give plastic sandwich bags of candies that are identified by flavor. The teams line up in columns, with their distributors standing about 10 feet away from the head of the line. On the signal the runner races to the team's distributor, receives a piece of candy, and races back to the team. The runner puts the candy in the mouth of the second person in line (the eater), who should not see the color of the candy. As soon as the eater recognizes the flavor, she whispers the name of the flavor to the runner, who returns to the distributor and whispers the flavor the eater guessed.

If the guess is correct, the runner races to the end of the line, and the eater then becomes the new runner. Play continues as before.

If the eater's guess is incorrect, the runner returns to the eater to ask for another guess, then returns to the distributor to repeat the guess in a whisper. (If all distributors give out the same flavors of candy at the same time, one team could hear the guess of another team if the guessing is not done in whispers.) Repeat this process until the correct flavor is guessed.

The team that is first to return its initial runner to the front of the line is the winner.
Greg Miller

School Craze

This relay race is a back-to-school event. Two teams race each other through a battery of school-like tasks, with each teammate responsible for one leg of the relay. Set up a large room with the necessary equipment and furniture (see diagram).

1. At the sound of the tardy bell, a team's first member sprints across the room, opens a combination lock (the combination is written on a piece of paper taped to the lock), then tags the second member.
2. This teammate picks up a large stack of books (make it challenging, but don't cause any hernias) and, stopping to pick up any that he drops, staggers across to table 1.
3. Once the books are plopped down, the third member may turn over a paper on which is printed a maze.

When the maze is completed, the teammate takes the maze to table 2, where a teacher (a sponsor) corrects it.

4. If the maze passes the scrutiny of the grader, the next teammate performs five push-ups, then races to tag the opposite wall before sprinting to table 3. (This is P.E.)
5. Now it's lunchtime. When the sprinter arrives at table 3, the fifth member waiting there must consume a burger and small Coke before dashing to the chalkboard and tagging the sixth teammate.

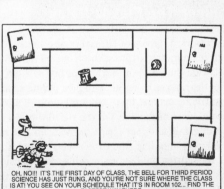

OH, NO!!! IT'S THE FIRST DAY OF CLASS, THE BELL FOR THIRD PERIOD SCIENCE HAS JUST RUNG, AND YOU'RE NOT SURE WHERE THE CLASS IS AT! YOU SEE ON YOUR SCHEDULE THAT IT'S IN ROOM 102... FIND THE FASTEST WAY THERE.

6. At the board, this member first solves a math problem previously written but covered until now, then copies a short phrase like "More homework" or "Biology's great!" (for composition) before racing to the next and final teammate on a waiting tricycle.

7. Time to go home. When the tricyclist is tagged, he pedals like mad for the finish line across the room. *Roger J. Rome*

Chewing Gum Relay

This is a relay race for two or more teams using sticks of chewing gum, work gloves, and shopping bags. Individual sticks of gum (wrapped) are placed inside the shopping bags, and each team is given a pair of work gloves. Players put on the gloves, run down to the bag, pull out a piece of gum, unwrap it and chew it (with the gloves on), run back, and then pass the gloves to the next person. The team that finishes first is the winner. *Jeffrey Collins*

Tapehead

Whether you play this game as a relay or a watch-and-cheer game, it's hilarious! Students wrap up their partner's head completely (obviously, making sure player can breathe) with masking tape, sticky side out. Then, in competition, the partial mummies run or crawl to an area where a variety of small, light objects is spread. They must lower their heads onto objects, "stick" 'em, then bring them back to where their partners remove the items and send their mummies back for another trip. The pair or team whose tapehead fetches the most items in a given amount of time wins.

Here are some common articles easily picked up by a tapehead: egg cartons, Styrofoam cups, plasticware, milk cartons, construction paper, shoe boxes, string, pie tins, paper clips, rubber bands, cotton balls, marshmallows, small stuffed animals, pencils, Q-Tips, inflated balloons, and paper plates.
Steve Bridges

Fruit Basket Fly-By

In this game, each team has two baskets, one filled with fruit at one end of the room, and the other empty at the other end of the room. Teams must compete to see who can be first to get all the fruit from one basket to the other. The trick, however, is that the fruit can only be transported by fruit fly players who fly by having their teammates carry them aloft and over a barrier of chairs or tables across the middle of the room.

Each team divides into halves. Then one-half goes to the side of the room with the full basket and one-half to the side with the empty one. On a signal one player from each team on the side with the full basket becomes a fly. They must tuck a piece of fruit under their chins, hold their arms out like wings, and be carried by their teammates up to a row of chairs or tables that separate them from the other side. There, the fly is carefully passed to the other half of the team waiting on the far side of the barrier. (After passing the fly over, carriers can crawl under or climb over the barrier to help carry the fly on the other side as well.)

Teammates on the other side then carry the fly to the empty basket, into which he drops the piece of fruit. The fly is let down, and immediately a new fly must be chosen to carry another piece of fruit, and so on until all the fruit has been transported. If necessary, after all the players have served as flies, some can repeat the role. If a piece of

fruit is dropped en route, the fly must land, pick it up, tuck it under her chin, and take off again as before. Team to complete the task first is the winner. *Lee Strawhun*

Connect Four

For this intimate relay either divide a large group into teams of five or six pairs, or ask the entire group to pair up and form a line of pairs. The first pair places a rubber playground ball between them at stomach level. To help keep the ball from falling and to help maintain balance, the two players place their hands on each other's shoulders. At a signal the next pair in line, in the same stance, tries to get the rubber ball from the first pair not with their hands, but by securing the ball between them at the stomach. The object is to pass the ball as quickly as possible from one set of people to the next without letting it fall. *Michael W. Capps*

Superhero Relay

Here's a game you can play next time you're doing a lesson on heroes. You'll need two "phone booths" (be creative; a couple of refrigerator boxes will work), two dolls, several tables, two masks, and two pairs of high-top tennis shoes.

Divide the group into two teams. Line them up about 50 feet away from the phone booths. The first two kids on each team run to their team's phone booth, go inside, and put

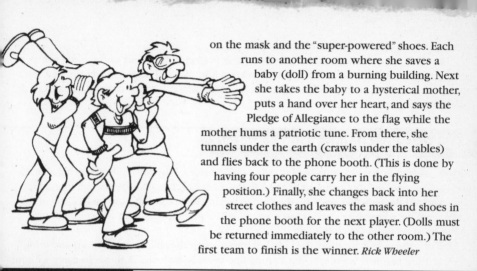

on the mask and the "super-powered" shoes. Each runs to another room where she saves a baby (doll) from a burning building. Next she takes the baby to a hysterical mother, puts a hand over her heart, and says the Pledge of Allegiance to the flag while the mother hums a patriotic tune. From there, she tunnels under the earth (crawls under the tables) and flies back to the phone booth. (This is done by having four people carry her in the flying position.) Finally, she changes back into her street clothes and leaves the mask and shoes in the phone booth for the next player. (Dolls must be returned immediately to the other room.) The first team to finish is the winner. *Rick Wheeler*

Retread Regatta

Get some bald tires, slice them in half like a bagel, fill each half with water, and—voilá—you have your own Ping-Pong ball regatta courses! Give each team its own water-filled tire, mark starting points with chalk, and begin the race. Each team member must take turns blowing the Ping-Pong ball once around the course. The first team that has every member round the tire wins.

Variations: Use sand instead of water, blindfold players so that they depend on their teammates' directions, or invent your own games! *Michael W. Capps*

Balloon Balance Relay

Form teams and give each team one baseball cap or painter's cap. The first player from each team dons the cap and balances an inflated balloon on the bill (bouncing on the bill is permitted). The players then walk to a point 10 feet away and back again while balancing the balloon on their hats. Then, using their hands, they pass the balloon and hat to the next players in line, who do the same thing.

A player whose balloon falls to the floor or is held up by any part of the body has to start over. (No fair blowing on the balloon to keep it in place.) The players on the first team to complete the circuit are declared the uncontested balloon balance relay champions of the world. *Michael Frisbie*

Sticky-Buns Balloon Burst Relay

Ask the kids to line up in pairs behind a line on one side of the room. On the other side of the room spread inflated balloons across the floor. Give each team of two a roll of masking tape, and tell the kids that on "Go!" they are to apply the tape around the midsection of the team member whose birthday is closest to today. The pair must use the whole roll of tape and it must be put on stick-side out.

When the tape is used up, the taped players must crab-walk to the balloons and bring back to their partners waiting at the starting line as many balloons as they can carry without using their hands. The waiting partner must then burst the balloons and save the ring part of the balloon (where you blow it up) to verify the number of balloons retrieved. Balloons popped by the sticky-bunned teammate don't count. The pair with the most rings wins.

This is a game to videotape. The kids are so dizzy from spinning around to get the tape on that they have a hard time doing the rest of the relay. *Keith Posehn*

Cake Relay

Each teammate runs a different leg in this relay, passing not a baton from runner to runner, but a cake (store-bought pound cake on a paper plate, or even Twinkies, melons, etc.).

The first leg could be an obstacle course of any kind; the second, a walking race (those who run are penalized by having to stand for 15 seconds); the third, a swim across the pool or waterfront in such a way that the cake stays above water; the fourth leg could require the runner to be blindfolded and directed verbally by a partner; the fifth, an all-out sprint for a quarter-mile or so.

After the last teammate crosses the finish line, the teams must eat the cake before the race is over. After all the wear and tear the cakes have endured—dropped, soaked, manhandled—this climax is hilarious. This game is a great group builder that requires teamwork, and it can be adapted to any situation. *Jon Davis*

Mummy Race

This relay requires teams to wrap up a teammate completely in cloth strips and then carry them up to the line and back. Each teammate is so wrapped and toted. First crypt of mummies finished with this sepulchral task wins. *Tom Jackson*

Pyramids By Braille

In this relay a blindfolded player must crawl 10 or 20 feet to where six Styrofoam cups lie. He must stack them up, pyramid fashion, before returning to his team and passing the blindfold off to a teammate. You, meanwhile, knock down each pyramid for the next players. *John Krueger*

Ski-Lays

Okay, so your church is in Mobile or Austin or Gila Bend, and half your group hasn't seen snow, not to mention played or skied in it. But don't let that stop you. Let the Denver and Seattle churches have their ski retreats—you can play these ski-lays (that's "ski relays") in your own Sun Belt gymnasium or youth room. Make skis from six foot (or longer) boards, and nail old Salvation Army shoes to them. Let these three snow-less ski-lays start you off.

* Ski Fill. At the starting line set up a small bucket of water for each team. At the opposite end of the room place a turn-around cone as well as an empty container. Give the first member of each team a paper or Styrofoam cup with a small hole in the bottom. On "Go!" the players must put on their skis, fill their leaky cups from the bucket, then ski their way to the cone, where they pour what remains of their water into the container. After they ski back to their own teams, the following players do likewise until one team's container is filled with water.

* Ski Plunger Toss. Seat a victim at the far end of the room from each relay starting line. The first player in each team must put on skis, pick up a plunger by the handle, grab a water balloon from a pile near each team, place the balloon in the plunger end, ski to a designated firing spot, and let fly at the victim (who, in all fairness to the shooters, must sit on her hands). Any skier who drops a water balloon en route forfeits his shot and instead returns to his line to let the next teammate go. The winning team is determined however you like—the first to wet the victim, the most hits in the least time, etc.

This game is appropriate for "honoring" a special adult or student. And you may find that most of the balloons don't have enough velocity to pop when they hit the victim. But don't tell the victims that—let them sweat it out.

* Balloon Racquet Relay. The object of this relay is to ski the length of the course (either around the cone or through an obstacle course), all the while keeping a balloon in the air with a racquet (tennis, badminton, racquetball, etc.). *Robert Marin, Jr.*

Buckle Up Relay

You'll need one bench seat per team for this game (the van variety, with seat belts attached); the removable seats from minivans work fine. Place the bench seats at a starting line. At a designated distance mark a finish line. Divide the kids into two (or more) groups. Place half of each team at the starting line and the other half at the finish line.

Instruct the first three at the starting line on each team to belt themselves into the van seats. On "Go!" the three belted-in players of each team stand to their feet and lumber toward the finish line, lugging the bench seat with them. When they arrive at the far line, they set the seat down, release the seat belts, and the second set of three strap themselves in and race back. Play continues until one team wins by releasing the belts of the final three racing members of the team. *Jerry Meadows*

Golf Ball And Plunger Cap Relay

Have the camera ready for this game! Make two teams and give a plunger (a plumber's helper) and a golf ball to each team. Ask the first player on each team to unscrew the wooden stick from the plunger and place the golf ball where the stick screwed in.

Players in this relay now must walk a prescribed course with the plunger cap on their heads and the golf ball balanced on the plunger cap. (The course can be simple—out 10 or 20 feet, around a chair, and back, for example.) Players who drop the ball return to their line and start over. For more of a challenge, place obstacles in the course, make the kids walk it backward, etc. *Rob Marin*

Long Jump Relay

Divide contestants into teams of six or eight, mark a starting line, and have kids stand by teams in single file behind it.

At the signal to go, each leader does a standing broad jump straight ahead (both feet must leave the ground simultaneously). The next in line then runs up to him, places his feet exactly where the leader's feet are, and does another standing broad jump. The third player runs up to the second and repeats the process. Likewise, each player in turn rushes forward and jumps from where the preceding player landed.

After the last player of every team has jumped, the total distance of each team is measured, and the farthest distance wins. *James C. Lutes*

Shovel Trouble

Shovel in hand, the first player on each team skateboards to a common pile of spuds at the other end of the lot, shovels up one potato, skates back to his team, deposits the potato in his team's box or basket, then passes both shovel and skateboard to the next teammate, who follows suit.

The game continues as long as the taters last; when they're gone, teams count what they've collected. The team with the most wins. Long-handled shovels work better than those with short handles— but the short-handled ones are more of a challenge to work with. *Michael W. Capps*

Bump Relay

Teams of 10 or so are seated in chairs lined up relay fashion. At a given signal, the first one in line leaves his seat and rushes to the back of his line, then—with some adept hip action— bumps the teammate off his chair to the right (see diagram). The bumped one moves forward a chair and bumps that teammate off to the left—and on to the front person, who runs around to the rear of the line and starts the process over again.

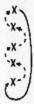

First team to return to its original chairs wins. *James C. Lutes*

Centipede Relay

Form equal teams of six to eight kids each and line up, alternating boy-girl. Instruct teams to back up to the wall at one end of the room, leaving three to four feet between the last person and the wall.

At the signal each team takes three short steps forward. As soon as the team has moved forward the last step, the first players in the lines break away to the right and run around their team three times as fast as possible, finally taking their place at the back of their team's line. Once in place, the runner yells, "Go!" and the process repeats with three more steps and new front runners. The relay continues until the line itself arrives at the youth leader standing at the other end of the room or crosses a line on the floor.

The room doesn't need to be large, since teams don't need that much room to move forward. They mainly need room on the sides of the lines to run around their teams without bumping into the competition. For every three steps forward, the team loses one body-space backward since the runner takes his place at the end of the line.

As a true test of speed and skill, each person tries to run around the team faster and faster. The key to winning this relay, however, is for everyone to press as close as possible to the people in front of and behind them. To make each line tighter, instruct players to grasp hold of the waist of the ones standing directly in front of them. (The kids may feel awkward doing this at first, but they'll comply as soon as they see their team losing the race.)

Be sure to point out that each person on the team may have to run several times in order for the entire team to reach the markers at the other end of the room. Also point out that the three short steps must be short. Demonstrate how they can move forward by simply placing one foot directly in front of the other and moving. *Michael W. Capps*

Indoor Obstacle Course

This relay game is best played by two or more teams. Because of the time necessary to complete the obstacle course, it's best to limit each team to six players or less.

Set up the course as shown in the diagram. Each player is given a soda straw. On the signal the first player from each team goes to the starting position to pick up one of five kernels of corn from a paper plate. The only way they can move the corn, however, is by sucking on the straw and creating a vacuum that holds the kernel while they walk over to a foam cup on the near side of a table five feet away. Once they reach the cup, they drop the kernel in it and go back for the next one, continuing until all the kernels have been moved. If a corn is dropped en route, the player picks it up again using the same method and continues.

Once all five kernels are in the cup, players must blow the cup cross the table (the wider the table, the better) and make it land in a box placed on the floor underneath the table's far edge. If the cup or any of the corn misses the box, the cup must be refilled by a designated assistant from the player's team and then

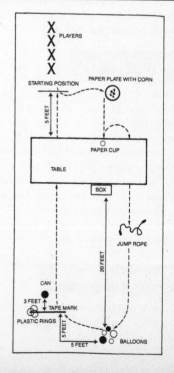

replaced on the table's edge. The player keeps trying until the cup and corn all fall into the box at once.

Next, players crawl under the table, grab a jump rope on the other side, and jump with it to a spot 20 feet away, where a pile of deflated balloons is waiting. They blow up one balloon until it bursts, then run to a tape mark on the floor five feet away. There they must pick up two plastic rings from the floor and toss them around a small can three feet away. (Empty bread crumb cans work well for this.) When the players have made a successful toss with both rings, they crawl back under the table and tag the next person (and probably collapse). The first team to complete the relay wins.

The game is as much fun to watch as it is to play, so kids who don't want to run the course may enjoy acting as assistants. Besides helping out with unsuccessful cup-blowing attempts, the assistants must also replace the cup on the table and the corn on the plate after the player has succeeded in that part of the relay.

As a variation you can use a stopwatch and allow individual players to compete against the clock. *June L. Becker*

Shirt Button Relay

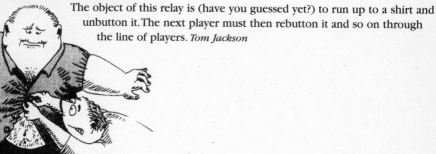

The object of this relay is (have you guessed yet?) to run up to a shirt and unbutton it. The next player must then rebutton it and so on through the line of players. *Tom Jackson*

Who says you need a pool or lake to enjoy liquid fun? These games are the ticket to refresh your kids on a hot summer day. Whether the games involve water balloons or Super Soakers, your group is guaranteed a sopping good time.

Laser Squirt

To get the same effect produced by expensive Laser Tag guns, try this version of tag. Use water-color markers to color a three-inch circle on a 4x6-inch card for each participant. Ask kids to bring their squirt guns and wear old shirts; you provide buckets for refilling. Tape a card to the chest of each player—and have at it! When the colored circle is hit with water, the color runs—and that player is dead and out of the game.

Form five-person color-coded teams and allow a few minutes of pregame planning before signaling hostilities to commence. The team with the most unsquirted members at the end of the time period wins. *Mark Adams*

Soaker

A hot outdoor afternoon is perfect for this water-balloon game. One person throws a water balloon high in the air and calls out another player's name (or number, if the group has numbered off). The called player must catch the balloon. If she succeeds at catching it unbroken, she gets a free shot at the thrower who called her name and gets her turn at throwing a water balloon up and calling another's name.

If a water balloon breaks during an attempt to catch it—well, that player gets soaked. And if a called-out player doesn't even attempt to catch it, turn the hose on him! *Chris Hayes*

Firefighter Water Wars

Add this to your list of outdoor, hot-weather water games. You'll need the cooperation of your local fire department, because the game requires a garden-hose adapter to a fire hydrant (fire departments have them). Or hook up your hoses to your normal water spigots if the water pressure is sufficient for this game.

Use the adapter to hook up three hoses (see diagram), and suspend an empty paint can on a pulley hanging from a wire or clothesline. Two teams will each use the water stream from their hoses to move an empty paint can toward the opposing team's end. Of course, both teams will have an immensely fun and soaking time of it. Form teams and conduct a tournament.
Bev Illian

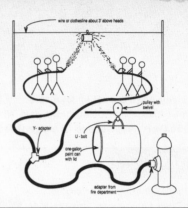

Jump Or Dive

This old favorite requires midair decision making. One at a time the young people take a nice, high bounce off the diving board. At the height of their jumps, you yell either "Jump!" or "Dive!"—and the young people must obey. You'll see some wild contortions as kids try to change their water-entry positions in a split second. If a hand hits the water first, it's ruled a dive; if a foot hits first, a jump.

If the kids get too good at second-guessing you, wait longer before you yell your command. Or really tie them in knots with an occasional "Jive!" *John Yarnell*

Search And Destroy

It's the last day of camp, the kids need an outdoor free-for-all, and—if you've been keeping track of team points all week—you need a final contest by which even the last-place team could conceivably catch up and win the entire week's competition.

So here's a combination scavenger hunt/water-balloon fight. First hide water balloons throughout the playing area (the more colors of balloons, the better). Begin the game itself by dividing players into teams and telling them the rules:

- After players find balloons, they must run, crawl, walk, sneak, or bluff their way back to "headquarters," where a sponsor tallies the balloons and records the score for the appropriate teams.
- Here's the twist: the point values of different balloon colors are not told to the players until the end of the game. (For example, yellow ones are 20 points each; blue, 15 points; red, 5 points; white, negative 5 points; pink, negative 10 points; three orange brought in on one trip by a player, 30 points; etc.).
- After the sponsor records players' points, the players are free to dispose of the balloons any way they want—and here's where the water-balloon fight begins.
- Players continue the process of finding, recording, and destroying until time runs out.

To keep the scorekeeper's skin dry, deduct big points for lobbing balloons at them. And when the melee is over, conduct a brief but crucial game to see which team can pick up the most balloon pieces. *David Holton*

Busted

Every group has at least some kids who would burst water balloons over their heads if they knew that a five dollar bill was in one of the balloons. So on a hot day, give your group a hilarious show, make someone five dollars richer—and maybe pull an object lesson from the silliness (what people will do for money, paying a price for getting what one really wants, etc.). Give volunteers only seven seconds; let more volunteers try their luck until the money is found. *Timothy Bean*

Missile Mania

For a massive-strike water-balloon fight, purchase two water-balloon slingshots and mark off a playing field (see diagram). At each end of the field is a launching pad where several designated players work the slingshot. In between the pads is a hand-to-hand open combat zone (the OCZ) where individuals may hand-throw water balloons at opponents. A player hit with a water balloon must go to the opposition's prison, located near the launching pad. There's also a safety zone at each end in which a player is immune from being taken prisoner and into which no opposition players may enter.

The object of the game is to hit a launcher on the opposition with a water balloon, thereby knocking out their launching pad.

After you divide the group into two teams, each team designates players who must remain at all times in their team's launching pad and use the water-balloon launcher to fire balloons over the OCZ in an attempt to hit any of the enemy launchers. Once a launcher is

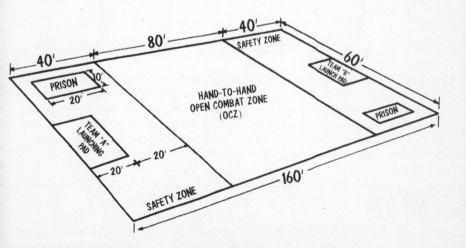

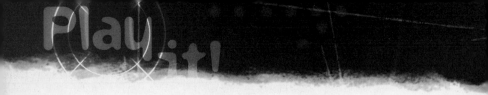

hit by a balloon, the pad is considered "knocked out," and the opposing team scores a point.

Other players engage in hand-to-hand balloon combat in the OCZ as they try to knock out a launching pad by throwing the balloons. In addition, they try to take enemy prisoners by hitting them in the OCZ. Those hit in the OCZ must remain in the opposition's prison until a knockout point is scored by their own team, at which time they are freed and may join the war again.

The first team to score 10 knockout points wins. *Gene Stabe*

Save Queen Bertha

Here's a water-balloon strategy game for outdoors.

Set up a battlefield (see diagram) and provide each team with an equal number of three kinds of balloons:

- Red balloons (or another specified color) are worth 100 points.
- Queen Bertha balloons are very large (purchase at party-supply shops) and are worth 1,000 points. Only one per team.
- A variety of smaller balloons have no point value but are weapons.

Teams begin the game in their own territory, attempting to advance their point water

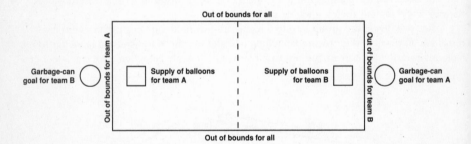

balloons beyond enemy territory and score them into the garbage can. Weapon balloons are thrown at carriers of point balloons; those carrying point balloons who get wet from an enemy's toss must relinquish their points to the enemy. This is the only way to steal points from the enemy—no physical contact or raiding of enemy supplies is permitted.

When about half the balloons are used, call a half-time so teams can reevaluate their strategies. When all the balloons are gone, the team with the most points in its garbage can wins. *John Stumbo*

Run 'N' Wet

Have your kids sit in a circle and number themselves off, then put a plump water balloon in the center of the circle. When the leader calls out two numbers, those two kids must jump up and run around the circle back to their own places—but no stopping yet. They must race through the empty spot they left to the water balloon in the middle.

Can you guess the rest? Yup—first one there gets to throw the balloon at the loser, who must stand still and not dodge it. *Lisa Nyman*

Waterball Samurai

The object of this wet warfare is to hit the other team's samurai with a water-soaked foam ball as many times as possible in one minute.

You will need a Wiffle bat, foam balls (at least six), water buckets (at least three), a step stool (from the water fountain), timekeeper and point counter, chalk or tape.

Make boundaries for the game by drawing or marking with tape a six-foot-diameter circle. Place the low stool in the center of the circle. Place three buckets on a line, 15 feet outside the circle's edge.

Divide the groups into teams of five or six players each, and ask each team to select one player to be the samurai. The samurai from the defending team stands on the stool in the center of the circle and may not step off the stool during the round. The remaining defending team members position themselves on the perimeter of the circle to defend their samurai from the waterballs. They can not move into the circle or beyond its perimeter. They must confine their movements to the edge of the circle. Their samurai, meanwhile, defends himself with a Wiffle bat to divert waterballs.

From behind the water-bucket line, the opposing team throws water-soaked foam balls at the samurai in the circle, attempting to hit him. If a thrown ball falls short of the circle, an offensive team member may run up to retrieve it and either carry it back to the line to throw it again or else toss it to one of the other team members already behind the line, who may then throw the ball at the samurai. Offensive players may not, however, enter the defending team's circle to retrieve any balls.

The round ends when one minute is up or all the waterballs are inside the circle. The offensive team gets one point each time they hit the samurai with a waterball or for each time the samurai steps off the step stool.

If you have more than three or four teams, you may want to get more foam balls and mark out more waterball courts so you can have several games going on simultaneously. Winners from each court can play one another in a championship game. *Doug Partin*

Fizzer Tag

Before you play this summertime, Laser Tag-type outdoor game, drill a small hole in the center of as many Alka-Seltzer tablets as you have kids, and then run a string through each tablet in order to hang it loosely around a player's neck. Have each player bring a squirt gun, provide several full buckets of water out-of-bounds for refills, and begin the game.

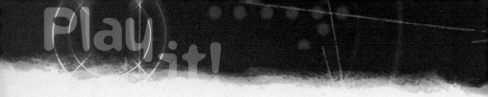
The object? When a player's Alka-Seltzer tablet gets hit enough and dissolves sufficiently to drop off the string, that player is out. To shorten the game, bring out the garden hose!
Jeff Minor

Giant Slip 'N' Slide Relay

With a 20X100-foot sheet of 6-mil plastic and a large, smooth grassy area, you're ready for fun! Spread out the plastic, hose it down, add some Johnson's Baby Shampoo to make it slick, and maybe some sprinklers along the sides to keep it wet.

Then start the relays: Team members must "swim" from end to end, be dragged by teammates (by hands or feet), or—the messiest of all—the watermelon relay. As racers run the course with a watermelon in their arms, adults pelt them with water balloons—as if the slippery plastic is not obstacle enough. When people drop their watermelons, they must pick up the pieces and continue the race.

When the free-for-all inevitably occurs, forbid the throwing of watermelon pieces (but not the stuffing of them in another's face). Free-for-all participants must stay on their knees.
Rick Brown

Ultimate Water Balloons

Played with a Frisbee, Ultimate Football is a game that combines teamwork with athletic prowess as the Frisbee is moved down the field in nonstop, continuous play with any one of a number of various twists to the game.

A favorite warm-weather variation is to substitute water balloons for the Frisbee. The referee should be supplied with 36 water balloons in advance (for an approximately 30-minute game), which are stored up and down along the sidelines (this allows for quick replacement of the two balloons that the ref always carries in his hands). The referee must hustle to get a balloon to the other team when one breaks as soon as possible so that play is not unduly interrupted. *Kevin Turner*

Water Balloon Soccer

Divide the group into as many teams of 10 to 15 as you can. Before the game, fill a minimum of three water balloons per team member. Also prepare one hat (or helmet) per team: With duct tape, affix tacks, point out, to a helmet or ball cap. The hat is then placed on an X on the ground about 20 feet from the starting line.

At a signal, the first person in line for each team runs to the hat and puts it on. The second person in the line lobs a balloon in the air in the general direction of the first player, who attempts to break the balloon with the hat. If the hat-wearing teammate misses, a second and third balloon are thrown. If he still doesn't puncture a balloon with his hat (and drenches himself in the process), he puts the hat down and goes to the end of his line—and the next teammate in line tries her luck. The first team that cycles the entire team through wins the event. *Brad Edgbert*

Fling 'Em

Divide lots of water balloons equally between four teams, and send each team to one of the corners in the playing area (see diagram.).

Each team selects two people to be its catchers, who take a garbage can with them into the catchers' area. When the game begins, teams attempt to lob (no line drives) their water balloons from their corners to their own catchers' garbage can in the middle of the playing area. The team with the most water in its can when all balloons are gone wins.

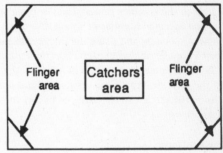

Remember these rules:
- Both catchers must hold the garbage can.
- Catchers can catch balloons from any team.
- No physical contact between opposing catchers is permitted unless they're vying for tossed balloons.
- Catchers cannot step out of their designated area.

Devise various ways of propelling the balloons to the cans: slingshots made from surgical tubing (make sure balloons are lobbed high into the air, not directed at the catchers), plastic throwers shaped like those used in jai alai, etc. *John Stumbo*

Taxi

This swimming pool game begins with two teams, each with an air mattress, on opposite sides of the pool. On "Go!" one member of each team straddles his mattress and paddles it around the pool. When the two players arrive back at their own starting points, they each pick up another teammate and make another lap—and this continues until the entire team is on the mattress.

The trick is mounting the mattress, especially with several kids already on it. There'll be a lot of thrashing and sputtering during this game! *Mark Ziehr*

Pistol Pong

After a few matches of Ping Pool, clear the plain, folding table and give a pair of kids squirt guns. Place a Ping-Pong ball in the center; the dueling players, armed with the guns, should try to squirt the ball off their opponent's end of the table. Balls that fall off the sides of the table are replaced from where they fell, and play is resumed.

For a variation, try playing doubles or set four players against each other on each side of a square table. And be prepared for the inevitable Fluid Free-For-All Finale. *Michael W. Capps and Michael Frisbie*

Sponge Dodge

In the heat of the summer, find a beach or open lawn, take along four or five five-gallon buckets and an equal number of sponges, and cool yourselves off with this game.

Mark out a circle and place the buckets around the perimeter. Half fill them with water, and drop a sponge or two in each. After the entire youth group gets in the circle, the leader soaks the first sponge and throws (aim below the head). Those who get hit join the leader around the edge, and the game continues until only one is left—the winner. Sponges that drop inside the circle can be retrieved by any thrower, but they must be dipped again before they are thrown.

Some variations:
- Reverse the game. That is, when someone is hit, the thrower joins those inside the circle. Last one on the perimeter loses.
- Play by teams. Time how long it takes for one team to get all members of an opposing team hit and out of the circle. Shortest time wins. Or set a time limit—the winning team has the most members still in the circle when the clock runs out.
- Run the game indefinitely, with no winners or losers. Begin the game with five inside the circle. Whoever makes a hit trades places with his victim.

Vernal Wilkinson

Volleyball Games

What self-respecting youth group doesn't like a good volleyball game? They'll go crazy for these bizarre variations of the sport. Regardless of your group size or space limitations, you'll find several volleyball mutations that work for you!

Volley Feetball

This volleyball variation will keep your group light-footed. You play it according to most of the traditional volleyball rules, except for one big difference—the net is lowered to within a foot or two of the floor, and players use only their feet to kick the ball under the net. Regular rules about out-of-bounds, team rotation, three-kick-per-team maximum, etc., apply.

Serving is like this: the players on both teams stand aside to let the serve reach the opposite team's back row—by traveling under the net.

After a back-row player has kicked it, players on both teams may move back into position and resume regular play. If a player in the front rows of the serving team touches a served ball before it goes under the net, it's side-out; if a player in the front lines of the receiving team touches the ball before it reaches his back row, the serving team scores a point. If the back row of the receiving team lets a served ball go out-of-bounds untouched, the serving team scores a point. When a player kicks the ball over the net, it's side-out or a point for the opposing team. Games are played to 7, 15, or 21, depending how much time you have.

Your kids will find the game a little tricky at first—they'll need to use the sides of their feet to kick with, soccer style. And you can always retreat to a smaller room with a Nerf ball and masking-tape boundaries. *Michael W. Capps*

Black-Light Volleyball

If you can black out your gym and obtain four black lights, your kids will love this game of guesswork and strategy. With orange or green fluorescent spray paint, spray a volleyball, the top of the volleyball net, and—if they wear old shoes—your kids' shoes. Cut up old white towels or sheets for headbands, and have the kids bring either white gloves or gloves you can spray-paint. Get people to hold the black lights instead of merely standing the lights up around the volleyball court—this way the holders can dodge a wild ball and lights won't be broken.

Then turn off the white lights, turn on the black lights, and play volleyball! Since headbands, shoes, and gloves are the only clues to players' positions, the teams will develop some strategy quickly—like slipping off their shoes in order to make a spike or momentarily hiding their heads and hands to outfox the opposition. *David Washburn*

Mega Volleyball

Here's how to play volleyball with an extra-large group (24 players or more at a time). You need three volleyball nets, four standards, lime or tape to mark the boundaries, two volleyballs, and a ref.

Place one pole in the center and the other three around it, so that the nets are stretched out from the center like spokes in a wheel (see the diagram). Make the boundary a circle so that each segment of the court is shaped like a pie slice (the three sections should be equal).

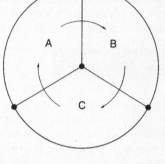

Play is similar to regular volleyball, except that the ball is not returned across the net to the serving team. Instead, it advances to the third team, who sends it on to the first team, thus moving either clockwise or counterclockwise around the circle. In the diagram shown, A serves to B, who volleys to C, who must get the ball back to A, and so on. To keep the game fun, don't allow spikes. For added excitement, get two balls going at once.

As in the regular game, errors includes misses, out-of-bounds volleys, more than three contacts with the ball by the same team before it crosses the net, and more than one contact with the ball in immediate succession by the same player. Scoring, however, is different from regular play in that 25 points are given for every error. Thus the team with the lowest score wins. *Ed Weaver*

Volleyslam

Volleyslam is a baseball-like game on a volleyball court, for two teams and any number of players. Home plate is under one of the baskets, and six bases are placed in the court's corners (see diagram). The defensive team scatters itself throughout the gym. The batter stands at home plate and bats the volleyball with a normal under- or overhand volleyball serve toward the far end of the court.

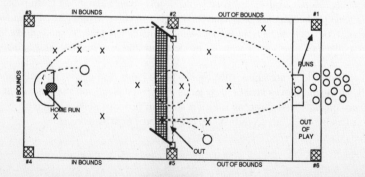

Outs are made only by hitting runners with the ball when they're between bases, or when a batted ball hits the net—not by catching flies. A base may hold any number of runners, and runners may pass each other. A home run is scored if a batted ball hits the backboard, rim, or net at the opposite end of the court. (Invent your own award if the ball goes into the basket—the feat certainly deserves one!)

Since there's no catcher, a thrown ball that crosses the home-base line is out of play—so runners must remain at the bases closest to them. Also notice that beyond the net, the area beyond the sidelines is still in-bounds.

All team members bat once and only once in each inning—outs retire base runners instead of determining inning length. *Phil Blackwell*

Headbangers Volleyball

This is played like regular volleyball, except that players can use only their heads to hit the ball.

The rules are as follows:
- A guy must hit the ball at least once every time the ball comes over the net, or that team loses the point.
- Each team can hit the ball five times to get it over.
- The ball can bounce once each time it comes over.

You may want to add these two rules:
- Guys can use only their heads to hit the ball.
- Girls can hit the ball according to standard volleyball rules.

Otherwise, the game is played by the normal volleyball rules. This game is as much fun to watch as to play. *Jack Hawkins*

Double-Vision Volleyball

Play volleyball with two balls. After both teams serve their balls simultaneously on the ref's command, each ball is played until it hits the floor or goes out of bounds. This means that either team can score with either ball, regardless of who served what ball. It also means that a team can score two points in a single, two-ball volley.

If you want to compensate for the power plays of stronger players, use plastic children's balls instead of standard volleyballs. *Keith King and Merle Moser*

Volloony Ball

On a basketball or volleyball court and across a volleyball net from each other, two opposing teams play a volleyball game—but with a weather balloon. Since getting control of the balloon is a ticklish matter, a team gets up to 10 hits before the balloon must be returned over the net. Similar to regular volleyball, a team earns points when its opponents (1) hit the balloon more than 10 times, (2) allow the balloon to touch the floor, (3) cause the balloon to hit the ceiling or lights, or (4) hit the balloon out-of-bounds.

You can make a weather balloon substitute by wrapping three lengths of masking tape around a balloon. *Phil Blackwell and Kevin J. Bueltmann*

Team Volleybasket

Divide the group into two teams on opposite sides of a volleyball net that is set in a basketball court. The serving team lines up along the sideline facing the server (see diagram), who does a normal volleyball serve from the normal serving position. After serving the ball, the server runs to the first person in line and gives that player a high five. That player in turn gives a low five to the next person, who gives a high five to the next, and so on to the end of the line. That last person then runs to the first person in the line and starts the process all over. Each time they complete the line (the slap-happy wave) they get one point.

Meanwhile, on the other side of the net, the volleyball is volleyed among the team members until it gets to the stationary shooter. It doesn't matter if the ball hits the ground during the volley. Players just pick it up and continue to volley to the shooter, who grabs the volleyball and shoots it, basketball-like, through the hoop. The shooter keeps at it until a basket is made, which also stops the action on the serving side of the net.

At that point the volleying team lines up facing the former shooter, who is now the server. The server makes a legal volleyball serve and starts the slap-happy wave while the receiving team volleys the ball back to its shooter. The serve alternates each time after the basket is made.

There are no points given for the basket—only for completing a slap-happy wave. The first team to 21 points wins. *Brad Edgbert*

Human-Net Volleyball

Use a light, large ball—like a beach ball—and divide into three teams (the third team composes the net). Mark or tape a two-foot-wide strip the net players must remain in; the other two teams may not enter the net's zone.

A regular volleyball game is then played, except that the net team plays too, earning points for each ball it can catch as the other two teams play. If the net merely knocks the ball out of play without catching it, no one scores. After each game teams rotate. *Terry Fisher*

Lottery Volleyball

This off-beat brand of volleyball adds the thrill of the unexpected. Divide into teams and position players conventionally. The referee should stand a few feet out of bounds near mid-court with a container of lottery tickets numbered 1 through 9 (have several of each number, and mix them up so that they can be drawn at random).

As the server serves, the referee draws out a ticket and calls out the number. The team receiving the ball must hit the ball that number of times (no more, no less) before returning it over the net. If the B team is successful, the serving team must do the same. Play continues requiring the same number of hits per play until a team fails. On the serve for the next round, a second ticket is drawn out and read, and play continues as before according to the number of hits required by the new ticket. Excitement will build on each play as team members count out hits, and you'll especially enjoy the groans when the referee calls out the dreaded number 1.

All other conventional volleyball rules prevail, but you might want to liven things up by using water balloons instead of a ball, or by playing flamingo style (on one leg). *Mark A. Hahlen*

Volleybowl

This fast-paced game is exciting for all ages, but especially for younger kids. You need two volleyballs, two bowling pins, and a large playing area (indoors or out).

Divide into two teams of equal size and have each one choose a "pin keeper." Then have each team line up, all facing the same direction, in two parallel lines about 15 feet apart. Set up a pin about 10 feet in front of the first person in each line, and have a pin keeper for each team stand behind his or her team's pin. Then give a volleyball to the first person in each line.

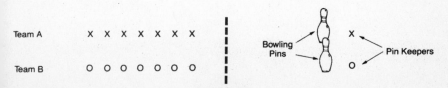

When a signal is given, the first person in each line attempts to knock down his or her team's pin, either by rolling or throwing the ball at it. If the pin is knocked down, the team gets a point. The pin keeper sets up the pin and returns the ball to the next person in line for play. If the pin is missed, no point is earned, and the pin keeper must return the ball to the next player in line. After each attempt, the player goes to the end of the line. Team members keep rotating in this way as fast as possible until the predetermined period of play (usually five minutes) is up. The team with the most points wins.

The excitement of the game is heightened if team members shout out their score after every successful attempt and when the two-minute and one-minute warnings are given. To add a wrinkle, use half-inflated balls or two balls for each team (a headache for the pin keepers); or have players throw the ball between their legs by bending forward.

Mark A. Hahlen

Ping-Pong Games

Beanbags for balls, books for paddles, and bowls of water on the table—these are just some of the twisted variations we've come up with for this beloved family game. In addition to these and other wacky new versions of traditional table tennis, you'll find several ideas for using Ping-Pong balls in other sports like baseball, basketball—and, yes, even polo.

Ping-Pong Blow

Players in this game spread themselves evenly around the edge of a large sheet, grab its edge, pull it taut (and keep it level), then attempt to blow a Ping-Pong ball off it. The players between whom the ball drops off the sheet are out, and the circle of players is gradually reduced.

Instead of a Ping-Pong ball, a balloon with a marble inside rolls around the sheet less predictably since the balloon isn't a perfect sphere. *David Washburn*

King Pong

If you have ever felt that the Ping-Pong table was just too short for your style of play, then this game could revitalize Ping-Pong for your group. Set two Ping-Pong tables end to end, and place the net as close to the middle as possible. Play regular rules or invent twists like relay-round-robin, multiple hits per side, or teams of four or more. The results are as fun to watch as they are to play. *Kevin Turner and the Camp McCullough staff*

Ping Pool

For a full hour of fun, try this Ping-Pong/pool table hybrid. First, borrow one of those six-foot-long fold-up tables from your kitchen or fellowship hall. Next, attach six Styrofoam cups along the edge of the table. Put one at each corner and one in the middle of each of the long sides—exactly like a pool table. Each cup should have its bottom punched out and replaced by a plastic Baggie, and the cups may need part of their top edges cut back and shaped in order to fit snugly to the table.

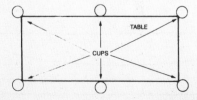

Now choose two teams of six students each and position them—on their knees, with their arms folded along the edge of the table, and with their chins resting on their folded arms. Place on the table 12 Ping-Pong balls—six white ones for one team, six red ones for the other. (Use a permanent marker to color the red ones so the color won't wear off during the game.) At the whistle each team tries to blow its balls into the table's pockets. The players' arms will keep the balls on the table. A few helpers can put balls back into play that hop the barricade of arms.

But be careful—only two balls are permitted in any pocket. A referee makes sure this rule is followed during play. The team that sinks its balls first wins.

Here are some variations:

- **Bumper Ping.** Place unopened, ice-cold cans of soda on the playing table (see below). Players must blow balls around the cans of pop to sink their balls in the pockets. The winning team gets the pop!

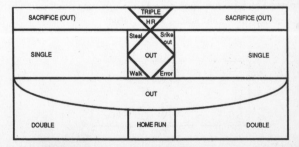

- **Tag-Team Ping.** Only one member from each of two competing teams plays at the same time. When a person has successfully pocketed one ball, he tags a team member (those waiting for their turns sit apart from the playing table), who then represents her team at the table. The game is over when a team has pocketed all six of its balls, one ball per person.
- **Challenge Ping.** Regular Ping Pool—except that only one ball of each color may roll into each cup.

Michael W. Capps and Michael Frisbie

Wall Baseball

During lock-ins, retreats, or any other times that find you indoors, Wall Baseball is safe, fun, and doesn't require typical baseball skills in order for kids of any age to have fun playing it. Here's what you'll need: a wall (preferably 15x10 feet, though any size will do), masking tape, labels, and a Ping-Pong ball and paddle. Use the masking tape and labels to duplicate this diagram on your wall:

Lay a home plate on the floor 20 feet or so away from the wall and a pitching rubber halfway or so between the wall and home plate.

Now to play. The pitcher tosses the Ping-Pong ball to the batter, who attempts to hit it with the paddle toward the wall. Where the ball hits the wall determines the play. If the

SACRIFICE (OUT)	TRIPLE		SACRIFICE (OUT)
	HR		
	Steal	Srike out	
SINGLE		OUT	SINGLE
	Walk	Error	
	OUT		
DOUBLE	HOME RUN		DOUBLE

The People Who Brought You this Book...
invite you to discover MORE valuable youth ministry resources.

Youth Specialties has three decades of experience working alongside Christian youth workers of just about every denomination and youth-serving organization. We're here to help you, whether you're brand new to youth ministry or a veteran, whether you're a volunteer or a career youth pastor. Each year we serve over 100,000 youth workers worldwide through our training seminars, conventions, magazines, resource products, and internet Web site (www.YouthSpecialties.com).

For FREE information about ways YS can help your youth ministry, complete and return this card.

Are you:　☐ A paid youth worker　　　☐ A volunteer　　　　　S=480001

Name_____

Church/Org. _____

Address ☐ Church or ☐ Home _____

City _____ State _____ Zip _____

Daytime Phone Number (_____) _____

E-Mail _____

Denomination _____ Average Weekly Church Attendance _____

The People Who Brought You this Book...
invite you to discover MORE valuable youth ministry resources.

Youth Specialties has three decades of experience working alongside Christian youth workers of just about every denomination and youth-serving organization. We're here to help you, whether you're brand new to youth ministry or a veteran, whether you're a volunteer or a career youth pastor. Each year we serve over 100,000 youth workers worldwide through our training seminars, conventions, magazines, resource products, and internet Web site (www.YouthSpecialties.com).

For FREE information about ways YS can help your youth ministry, complete and return this card.

Are you:　☐ A paid youth worker　　　☐ A volunteer　　　　　S=480001

Name_____

Church/Org. _____

Address ☐ Church or ☐ Home _____

City _____ State _____ Zip _____

Daytime Phone Number (_____) _____

E-Mail _____

Denomination _____ Average Weekly Church Attendance _____

BUSINESS REPLY MAIL
FIRST-CLASS MAIL   PERMIT 268   HOLMES PA

POSTAGE WILL BE PAID BY ADDRESSEE

YOUTH SPECIALTIES
P.O. BOX 668
HOLMES, PA 19043-0668

NO POSTAGE
NECESSARY
IF MAILED
IN THE
UNITED STATES

BUSINESS REPLY MAIL
FIRST-CLASS MAIL   PERMIT 268   HOLMES PA

POSTAGE WILL BE PAID BY ADDRESSEE

YOUTH SPECIALTIES
P.O. BOX 668
HOLMES, PA 19043-0668

ball hits the single area, for example, then the batter has hit a single and may proceed to first base. Defensive players position themselves wherever they think they can catch fly balls or prevent balls from hitting the game wall.

Other rules:
* All players—pitcher, batter, everyone—play on their knees at all times.
* Balls that hit the floor or ceiling before hitting the wall are ruled as outs.
* There's no base running necessary in this game—all outs are force outs. Runners (so to speak) advance around the bases on their knees and consequently very slowly.
* No fast pitching.

A plate ump is usually a good idea for calling obvious strikes and deciding where on the wall the ball hits in the case of a dispute. Play as many innings as you want. *Brett C. Wilson*

Ping-Pong Home-Run Derby

You can play this all-or-nothing version of baseball with just a handful of kids, a fair-sized room, a Ping-Pong ball, and a paddle (the bat). Set four or five folding tables on their sides as a playing-field fence (see diagram). Use masking tape to form a home plate and two foul lines.

Now for the rules:
* All players must play on their knees.
* There are no strokes, no balls, no base hits—just home runs or outs. The batting team tries to hit home runs. Any Ping-Pong ball that clears the fence without touching the floor or ceiling is a home run and scores a run. If a hit ball touches the floor or ceiling, or is caught or swatted down by a fielder, the batter is out. Foul balls are played over.
* The fielding team, which plays along the inside of the fence, tries to swat a hit Ping-Pong ball down before it flies over the fence.
* Each team gets three outs; play as many innings as you like. The pitcher can be a sponsor who pitches to both teams or a member of the fielding team. You may choose to have an umpire and scorekeeper.

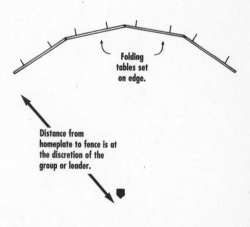

Folding tables set on edge.

Distance from homeplate to fence is at the discretion of the group or leader.

Brett C. Wilson

Power Pong

First, clear the room of all breakables. Set up the Ping-Pong table and put out at least four paddles. Start the Ping-Pong game, two (or up to six) to a team. Serving and scoring are according to standard Ping-Pong rules. Neither players nor their paddles can cross the net.

Now for the power. As in volleyball, each side is permitted as many as three hits before returning the ball across the net. A player cannot hit the ball twice consecutively. Walls, ceilings, and bodies are all in play. The ball is dead when the ball touches the floor, and the point goes to the opposition.

Like volleyball, the key is in teamwork—accurate sets, smashing returns. Better have a few extra balls for this one. *Mick Hernandez*

Ping-Pong Soccer

From six to 16 people can enjoy this indoor version of soccer. The rules are the same as regular soccer—except you play with a Ping-Pong ball, there are no boundaries, and the goals should be made much smaller.

Although the size of the field is small, the game plays amazingly like soccer because a well kicked Ping-Pong ball travels only 15 to 20 feet. Have plenty of Ping-Pong balls—they tend to get squashed on a blocked shot. Penalize a ball-squashing team by awarding the opposing team a free kick at the goal. *Elliott Cooke*

"Wide games" are what we call games requiring teams to strategize, organize, and assign tasks. They call for more than the usual planning, stealth, and skill. Most wide games—sometimes called "adventure games"—have a theme, like spies or secret agents, armies at war, and the like. Most require a good deal of space, such as an open field or a wooded area with places to hide.

3-D Stratego

Here's a combination of Capture the Flag and the board game Stratego, for which you'll need the standard Capture the Flag equipment—two flags and a big area with plenty of hiding places—as well as a couple decks of playing cards (or Rook cards).

After two teams are formed and they both hide their flags, give each player a playing card—a heart or diamond to Red teammates, and a spade or club to Black teammates. The cards determine a player's rank—the king is the highest; then the queen; on down to the ace, which is lowest. The ace, however, is the only card that can beat a king.

Once play begins, both teams try to capture the opposing team's flag, according to normal Capture the Flag rules. When a tag occurs, both players reveal their cards. The highest-ranking card wins and continues playing, but the losing player goes to "Central Exchange"—somewhere central in the game—in order to exchange her card for another (of the same color). Only then can that player rejoin the game. If both players in a tag have identical rank, both must go to the Central Exchange and exchange their cards for new ones.

The winner is the first to capture the other's flag and return it to home territory.

For variety, you can make all 10s bombs, which can blow up all other cards. All fives can be members of the bomb squad, who are the only ones able to defeat the 10s.
Rauel Fedlheizer

Mission Impossible

This game requires a large field, campgrounds, or woods. The object is for the members of two teams to find their team's secret "M" bomb (watermelon) that was stolen and hidden by enemy agents (sponsors). In the process, players shoot each other with squirt guns filled with disappearing ink.

Scattered evenly throughout the playing area are six DMZs. Each of these demilitarized zones are about 25 feet in diameter (marked with flour or lime) and serve as infirmaries and ammunition depots. They're each equipped with a staff person, a pail of disappearing ink (read instructions and dilute properly), and—at the beginning of the game—a third of a team's squirt guns.

Players should wear light-colored shirts in order for the disappearing ink to be seen; teams should be visually distinguishable—different colored squirt guns, armbands, etc.

The game begins this way: While students are gathered at HQ (a meeting hall or other central place) to receive their instructions, a staff member hides the two watermelons in the playing area.

Rules the kids need to hear include these:
- The purpose is to find their team bomb and return it to HQ.
- When players are shot on their shirts, they are considered wounded and must go to the nearest DMZ and wait for the ink to disappear. The attendant staff member then permits recovered players to rejoin the battle.
- While players are refilling their guns in the DMZs, they cannot be shot.
- Recovering players in the DMZ cannot refill their guns, but must wait until they are released and can go to another DMZ to refill.
- If a player finds the bomb but is shot as he's carrying it back to HQ, he must set it down gently (broken melons lose the game for the team that breaks them) and go to the DMZ as usual. Then either a teammate may pick up the bomb and attempt to finish the mission, or an opponent may take the bomb to hide it again.

After these rules are explained to the players, each team has five minutes to discuss its strategy. You may also want to have the initial squirt-gun filling done ahead of time by staff or by a few team members sent to the DMZs while the teams are laying battle plans. You'll probably need a whistle or bell to begin the game and then end it—perhaps after 30 minutes of playing if neither team has won by then.

Afterward, enjoy the watermelons! *Vaughn VanSkiver and Steve Robertson*

Jailbreak

Have a large group, a large building with several entrances and a dark night? Then you're set for Jailbreak!

The object is to break into the building, read a message that clues you in to the whereabouts of the treasure, find the treasure, and deliver it to a predetermined leader—all without being caught by guards and imprisoned.

First, divide any number of young people into two teams. Then choose guards: They must be adult leaders or unbiased kids, for the guards must be absolutely neutral, arresting members of both teams impartially. They will patrol the building in pairs, clockwise—never counterclockwise in order to catch players—arresting anyone they can shine their flashlights directly on. When this happens, the guard shouts, "Stop for identification!" The player must stop in his tracks and allow himself to be escorted to jail, where he must remain for 10 minutes or until another player breaks him out.

A jailbreak is achieved when a player enters the jail, tags a prisoner, and both of them flee—all without being detected by guards.

What keeps this game active is this: A player earns 100 points for breaking anyone out of jail—even members of the opposing team. Like the guards, the jailer must be an impartial player who never alerts guards, but merely verifies that jailbreaks are legitimate, tallies points for both teams, and settles any disputes.

For more suspense, place a searchlight on the flat roof of the building, and rotate it slowly or turn it on for a few seconds every five minutes or so.

What Jailbreak requires is trust and common honesty. When a patrolman gets you in his beam, for example, the player needs to freeze for the game to continue enjoyably. Prisoners must cooperate as they are escorted to jail. Games with trust factors teach kids the benefits of honesty and fair play—and are great discussion starters for later, too. *Steve Smoker*

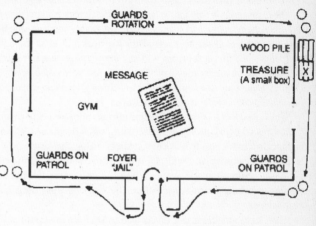

Murder Mystery

- **Directions.** In this game the kids are detectives questioning suspects in an effort to find the killer of Mr. John Stone. The five suspects (Mr. Mun, janitor; Steve Stone, John's brother; Sam Swade, lawyer; Mrs. Stone, John's wife; and Ms. Wright, secretary) are prepared ahead of time to act their parts using the scripts provided (pages 95-100). They should come in costumes—the secretary looking seductive, the lawyer shady, the janitor in overalls, and

so on. The remaining players are divided into groups of five or six detectives and will attempt to solve the mystery by working within their groups.

The game begins with everyone seeing the scene of the murder (see "Setting Up the Murder Scene" on page 94) and hearing the scripted Opening Comments to Detectives given by the host (on page 95). After the opening, each suspect leaves for a separate room, and the groups of detectives move from room to room questioning them (one group in a room at a time, with a time limit of five or 10 minutes per visit). Groups may visit any suspect as many times as they like.

At the conclusion of the game, all groups return to the scene of the murder and write on a piece of paper who they think killed John Stone and how and why they think the murder took place. The game leader then reads all the solutions offered by the kids as well as the solution provided (see "Solution to Murder Mystery" on page 100).

The success of this game lies with the actors playing the five suspects. Skillful youths may play these parts, but it may work out better with adults. Before the game is played, the suspects meet to listen to each other's scripts and hear the solution to the mystery. During the game itself the detectives will ask many questions not covered by the scripts, and although the suspects may say, "The question you asked is not relevant," suspects may also ad-lib as long as it does not conflict with or give away the solution. This can only be done if they already know each other's material.

Each suspect's script is divided into an alibi and one or more confessions. Suspects tell their alibis to every group, but they only offer their confessions if the detectives can prove (by quoting evidence from other suspects) that the suspect being questioned is lying. For example, many suspects will claim that they were not at the office that night, but the janitor will place them all at the scene. When the detectives tell the suspects that the janitor testifies to seeing them at the office, the suspects spill their guts, giving the second part of their scripts.

The suspects must use discretion in their answers. If they are stingy with information, the game will go on too long; if they too readily tell all, the detectives will catch on too quickly. The janitor's first part is rather simple, but the key is when he says that he found the body while checking to see if John and his friends had left. The janitor gives his second part only when the detectives ask if he saw others there.

- **Setting Up the Murder Scene.** The scene is a business office containing a desk and a table (or bookshelf) holding an aquarium. The office is topsy-turvy from an apparent struggle. Papers and file folders are strewn about the room and on the desk. Clearly visible among the papers on the floor is a broken picture frame containing a photo of the actress who plays the part of Mrs. Stone. On the desk is an agenda showing meeting times as follows: secretary 8:00 p.m., Steve Stone 8:30 p.m., Sam Swade 9:15 p.m. The aquarium is tipped over with the gravel falling off the edge of the table. Add some broken glass around it, and on the floor beneath it place some dead fish (from a local pet store's casualties) or cutouts of fish. Also below the aquarium trace the outline of a person with either chalk or masking tape to indicate where the body was found. Add some ketchup, broken glass, and water around the outline of the head. *John McLendon*

Opening Comments to Detectives

This is the office of John Stone, who was murdered last night. The janitor found him on the floor at 10:00 p.m. The cause of death was a blow to the back of his head, and the time of death was between 8:00 and 10:00 p.m. From the agenda on the desk, we know that he was working late and was to see his secretary at 8:00 p.m., his brother Steve Stone (who was his business partner) at 8:30 p.m., and his lawyer Sam Swade at 9:15 p.m. We have all three of these people here for you to question. We also have Mr. Stone's wife here, as well as the janitor who found his body.

Your job is to find out who killed John Stone and how and why they did it. That is, by evidence at the scene and from what you learn from the suspects, you must prove who the murderer is, the motive for the murder, and the method of the murder. Once you know this information, write it on a paper. We will read all your conclusions at _____, then I will tell you who is right.

You are investigators. When you get some evidence, use it to get more information. One or more of these people will be lying, but if you confront them with evidence, they will come clean. For instance, if you find out that one of the suspects made a death threat, do not say to that person, "did you say you would kill John Stone?" Say instead, "I have a witness who will testify that you said you were going to kill John Stone."

The suspects will not have answers to all your questions. If they seem to be making up answers to some of your questions, it is not always a clue that they are lying. They may be trying to give an appropriate answer that will not at the same time lead you off track. They may also decline to answer saying that your question is not relevant to the case.

MRS. STONE, JOHN'S WIFE

Alibi: All I know is my husband was a good man, and I don't know why anyone would want to kill him. I was home all night long until 10 o'clock when the police called and (she beings to cry) told me John had been killed.

Confession: I had a phone call from someone. He would not give his name, but he said my husband was having an affair with his secretary. I had suspected it for a long time and had told several of my friends that if I found out it was true I would kill him. When I got the call I went to his office. I was very angry, but I was not going to kill him. When I got there, the place was a mess. Papers were everywhere, my picture was smashed, and the carpet was soaked from the broken aquarium. It looked like there had been a terrible fight. John was (attempting to retain emotional control of herself) lying there-blood all over the back of his head. I can still see him in my mind-his blank expression and all those fish wiggling around him. I couldn't have killed him. I loved him.

MR. STEVE STONE, BROTHER TO JOHN

Alibi: I had a meeting set up with my brother to finalize some papers on an account we had been working on. I was to meet him at his office at 8:30, but I had an emergency come up and was not going to be able to make the meeting. I called several times to tell John I wasn't coming and that he should make whatever decisions had to be made and that I'd back whatever he though was best, but I never got an answer at his office. I never left my office. In fact, I was still there when the police called to tell me John had been murdered.

Confession: Yes, I was at John's office at 8:30 for the meeting. When I walked in he was on the floor. There were signs of a struggle-some pictures were broken, some papers were scattered on the floor. I went to look at John, and there was a small pool of blood from a blow to the back of his head. I would have called the police, but my brother and I had been having some problems.

You see, John was greedy for power and money (getting angry now). He was trying to cut me out of the business. I had been working with our lawyer, Sam Swade, to steal the control of the company from John. There were some papers in John's office we had falsified, and I though it would be best if I got them out of the office before I called the police. But I couldn't find them. That's when I knew Sam Swade must have killed John. He was a crook to begin with, and there's not telling what kind of deals he's been pulling. I didn't know what to do, so I left and went back as if I'd never left there, and waited until the police called.

I didn't kill him. He was already dead when I got there. I couldn't kill him. He was my brother! But I bet my life Sam Swade is behind this.

MS. SANDY WRIGHT, SECRETARY

Alibi: I came by the office at 8 o'clock to drop off some papers for Mr. Stone. He needed them for some meetings he was having that evening. I was only there for a minute. He was on the phone, so I left them on his desk. He said thanks and I left. That's all I knew until the police called me at my home around 10 o'clock to tell me Mr. Stone was dead.

Confession: Yes, I was having an affair with Mr. Stone. When I came in to drop off the papers, he told me it was over–I was being let go Monday and he told me not to ever set foot in the place again. He treated me like some undesirable business deal. I was hurt and angry. I pulled his wife's pictures off the wall and broke them. Then I started yelling at him. He started toward me from around the desk. I didn't even want him to touch me, so I pushed him away, and he tripped over the lamp cord and hit his head. Then he just laid there and didn't move at all. I didn't mean to kill him. It was an accident (starts crying). You can ask the janitor. He heard the pictures breaking and heard the yelling and came into the office just as John fell and hit his head. He told me to go home and he would make it look like a break in and robbery. I did it because I looked so guilty and was afraid. I swear I did not mean to kill him.

MR. SAM SWADE, LAWYER

Alibi: I was scheduled to meet with John Stone at 9:15 to finalize the signing of some business papers that he and his brother were working on. But my paging service left a message with me that someone had called and cancelled the appointment. She didn't say who called—I just assumed that it was John. The message said the meeting would be rescheduled for the next day sometime, so I never went to John's office. The first thing I heard was when the police called me at home around 10 o'clock.

Confession: Yes, I did go to John's office at 9:15. When I walked in, John was lying on the floor. Things were messed up—papers all over the floor, some pictures were broken. I went around to look at John closer. There was a little blood on the floor, which seemed to come from the back of his head. I could tell by looking at him he was dead.

I was going to call the police, but first I had to check on some records. Steve Stone had been having some power struggles with his brother, and I had helped him falsify some records so he could gain more power in the company. When I looked, though, the records were gone. Steve was the only one who knew about them, so I knew he had to be the one who took them. I knew he was hungry for power. In fact, although I can't prove it, I think he was also blackmailing John.

Two days before his death John told me somebody was blackmailing him. He had been having an affair with his secretary, Sandy Wright, and told me someone was getting him for big bucks to keep it from his wife. He asked me for advice on how to get out without legal problems. I told him the first step was to break the relationship with Ms. Wright and get her as far away from him as possible. In fact, he was going to do that when she brought the papers by the night of his murder.

I'm innocent. I didn't kill John Stone. He was dead when I got there. The more I think about it, the more the finger points straight at Steve Stone.

MR. MUN, JANITOR

Alibi: I had been working in the building like I always did. Mr. Stone told me he had some late meetings, which was not uncommon. So about 9:55 I went by to make sure he and his friends were gone before I locked up. When I walked in, it was a pitiful sight. Someone had torn the place to bits, and Mr. Stone was dead on the floor. As soon as I saw him, I called the police.

Confession A: *[Use the following speech only if the detectives ask who you saw come in]* Well, his secretary came by to drop off some papers. I was cleaning the hall. She went in and came right back out. Then a while later I saw Mr. Stone's brother going through the main lobby. I'm not sure how long he was there because I didn't see him leave. A little later I saw Mr. Stone's lawyer, Sam Swade, getting out of his car in the parking lot, but I didn't see him leave either. Mrs. Stone's wife must have also been there because her coat was on the rack when I went to lock up around 9:50. But it wasn't there when I had cleaned the hall at 8 o'clock.

Confession B: Okay, I was cleaning the hall when Ms. Wright came by with the papers. She went into the office. After a little while I heard glass break and some yelling. I came down the hall and walked into the office. As I did I saw Mr. Stone coming around the desk toward Ms. Wright. As he got to her, she pushed him away and he tripped and fell backward. His head hit the aquarium, and it busted everywhere. Then he fell to the floor. I checked him for his pulse, but he was dead. I knew it was an accident, so I told Sandy-ah, Ms. Wright-to go home, that it was an accident, and that I would make it look like someone else had robbed the place. She left, but before I could do anything, Mr. Stone's brother showed up. He saw his brother, then snooped around the place looking for something. He finally left. When I was sure he had gone, I started again to make the place look like a robbery. But then Mr. Swade came down the hall. He looked all over the room also, but didn't leave with anything. Not long after that Mr. Stone's wife came and then ran out. After that I just messed the place up a little and called the police. I was only trying to help Ms. Wright.

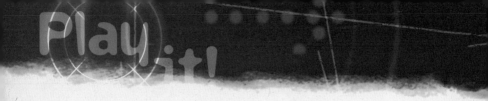

SOLUTION TO MURDER MYSTERY

John Stone was in his office at 8 o'clock when his secretary Ms. Wright (with whom he had been having an affair) came in. On the counsel of his lawyer, John broke off the relationship with her and let her go as his secretary to avoid being blackmailed. She reacted violently, smashing the picture of John's wife. John came around the desk to try and restrain her, but she pushed him away. He tripped, fell backward, and hit his head on the aquarium stand. He fell unconscious on the floor, but was not dead. The janitor came in just as John hit his head and fell to the floor. He saw it was an accident and told Ms. Wright to go home and he would make it look like a robbery.

Before he was able to do this, however, Steve Stone came in. Seeing the mess and his brother on the floor, he went to the file and took out some papers he had falsified so that he could steal the company from his brother. He felt that if they were found, it would make him look guilty of killing John. He was sure that the lawyer had killed his brother and was going to pin it on him.

He then went back into his office and waited there as if he had never left.

Again the janitor was unable to finish making the place look like a robbery because the lawyer came in. He also looked for the paper that Steve had taken. When he could not find them, he figured that Steve was the murderer and that he was going to use the papers to frame him. So he also left and created an alibi.

Soon after this John's wife received a call telling her that he was having an affair. When she came down she was out for blood, but it had already been shed. When she saw the mess she was afraid that it would look like she had indeed killed her husband in a fit of rage. She also left, but what she saw was the main piece of evidence. She said that the fish were alive ("wiggling around him") at 9:50, which meant that the aquarium could not have been broken by the secretary at 7 o'clock. However, no one else had mentioned the aquarium being broken-except the janitor. Mr. Mun said Ms. Wright pushed John, and his head hit the aquarium, breaking it.

When Sam Swade left John's office, the janitor again tried to mess up the room. His intent was not simply to make it look like a robbery, but to really rob John Stone. Since he believed his blackmail scheme was already destroyed (Mr. Mun thought John was dead), he decided to remove the safe keys from John's body, clean the place out, and pin the murder and robbery on Ms. Wright, Steve Stone, or Sam Swade. But as he searched John's pockets for the keys, John began to wake up. Mr. Mun picked John up enough to strike his head again, this time truly killing John Stone.

To cover his tracks, he called John's wife and told her John was having an affair. He knew she suspected it and had overheard her threatening John in the office. He did not anticipate that it would be her testimony that would put him away.

10

All of the games in this chapter are designed for use with groups in a confined area, such as the living room of someone's home, and require relatively little physical activity. They are ideal for parties or for warm-ups before a meeting or activity.

Also included are thinking or word games that require answering questions, table games that are usually played around card tables, and mind reading games that require some mental gymnastics to figure out how the game is played.

Candy Quiz

Hand out the quiz on page 102 as an individual challenge or a small-group project. Each phrase is a clue to the name of a candy bar.

Candy quiz answers:

1. Musketeers
2. Twix
3. Mounds
4. Milky Way
5. Red Hots
6. Mars
7. Hollywood
8. O'Henry
9. Snickers
10. Butterfinger
11. M & M's
12. Clark Bar
13. Baby Ruth
14. 5th Avenue
15. Kiss
16. Payday
17. Slow Poke
18. Black Cow
19. Junior Mints
20. Milk Duds
21. Bit-o-Honey
22. Almond Joy
23. Reese's Pieces
24. Sweetarts
25. Rolos

Roger Haas

Candy Quiz

1. A famous swashbuckling trio of old: _____
2. Elmer Fudd's sleight-of-hand or magical maneuvers: _____
3. Places of interring enemies of those who tend and drive cattle and who are usually mounted on domesticated, large solid-hoofed, herbivorous mammals: _____
4. A broad, luminous, irregular band of astral lights that encompasses the stellar sphere: _____
5. Crimson-colored libidinous cravings: _____
6. A celestial body fourth in order from the sun, conspicuous for the redness of its light; its planetary symbol is: _____
7. The hard, fibrous xylem substance produced by the Aquifoliaceae family of shrubs and trees, characterized by their thick, glossy, spiny-margined leaves and usually bright red berries: _____
8. Author William Sidney Porter's pseudonym: _____
9. Multiple expressions of mirth, joy, or scorn in a covert or suppressed manner: _____
10. An idiom, used here singularly, employed to describe one whose dexterous deficiency denies proficiency in getting a grip on goods: _____
11. Possessive clone alphabetical characters: _____
12. A saloon named after the newspaper-reporter alias of a superhero: _____
13. Childhood name of a former renowned baseball player whose strike-out record is recondite: _____
14. Celebrated street in the Big Apple: _____
15. Labial massage: _____
16. The 24-hour part of the week set aside to compensate for labor or toil: _____
17. A sluggish jab: _____
18. Ebony-colored country critter: _____
19. Subordinate spices or seasonings: _____
20. Lactic flops: _____
21. A morsel of regurgitated sweet viscid material from the social and colonial hymenopterous insect: _____
22. The jubilant sensation of an ellipsoidal and edible nut: _____
23. Label on the body bag containing the remains collected after a cat named "Reese" was run over by a mower: _____
24. Dissonant confectionery mixture of dulcet and piquant seasonings: _____
25. To rotate several members of the cylindrical-shaped component of the vowel family: _____

Four On A Couch

This is best played with at least 20 players. Write everyone's name on a slip of paper, one name per slip, and place the papers in a container.

Now sit everyone in a circle, with the couch (or four chairs) as part of the circle. Two boys and two girls (alternating) should sit on the couch. The teens sitting on the floor in a circle should leave one empty space.

The goal is to fill the four spaces on the couch with either all boys or all girls.

Once your teens are all situated, have each player draw a name from the container. Then start with the person sitting to the right of the open space: he calls the name of anyone in the group. Whoever holds the slip of paper with that name on it moves to the open spot and trades slips with the person who called the name. The play continues, with the person who now sits to the right of the vacant spot. (Pay attention, especially to the last name called.) Other players may not give hints to the player whose turn it is. *Christopher Graham*

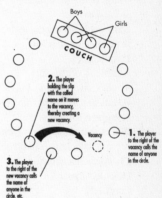

Drawing In The Dark

In a dark room or with tightly closed eyes, participants must make a pencil drawing of a scene you describe to them.

Give every student a sheet of paper and a pencil. The idea is to direct them to draw portions of the entire picture in the dark so they can only guess at the accurate position to place an object.

Turn out the lights, then tell them to draw, say, a house in the middle of the paper. Then ask them to place a tree to the left of the house. Then add a snowman to the right. Now put a chimney on the roof of the house. Draw a mailbox by the door. Draw a boy by the snowman. Put a scarf on the boy. Put smoke coming out of the chimney. Draw a dog by the tree. Put curtains in the window, a hat on the snowman, a nest in the tree, a flag on the mailbox, and so on.

Post the masterpieces at the end of the game. *Lyn Wargny*

Find The Mailman

Tell the kids that it's April 15 and your tax forms need to get to the post office. Hold up a fat envelope and tell them you have the tax forms, but they have to figure out who the mailman is.

Ask everyone to sit in a circle. Give one player your envelope of tax forms and ask her to wait outside of the room. Now choose another person to be the mailman, and assign him a mannerism like one of these:

> Blinks a lot
> Answers questions by saying "Awesome!"
> Sits with legs crossed
> Arms are always folded
> Taps his foot
> Name is Mr. Mailman
> Sleepy, yawns
> Ends each sentence with "...you know?
> Scratches head a lot
> Laughs a lot
> A Bible is on his lap
> Always says "I don't know"
> Hands are in a praying position
> Coughs a lot
> Wears someone else's jacket
> Always asks if you need some stamps
> Twiddles his thumbs
> Licks his lips a lot
> Can't talk
> Shifts in his chair a lot
> Puts his arm on his neighbor's chair
> Smiles a lot
> Ends each sentence with "Have a nice day!"
> Hands have both index fingers pointing at you
> Winks at you

Set a time limit (one or two or three minutes, depending on the size of your group) and a limit on how many questions the tax-envelope holder ("It") can ask each student in the circle—say, three questions per player—by which time "It" must put the envelope in the mailman's hand. When "It" returns to the room, suggest to her that she pay attention to body language as well as peculiarities in how kids answer her questions. Players must respond honestly to questions. *Mark Schwartz*

High Roller, High Writer

Get a small group of kids around a table, and place in the middle one die and one pencil. Provide a sheet of paper for each player. Determine who plays first; then begin. The first player rolls the die once, then passes it clockwise so the next player can also roll once before passing the die on.

When a player rolls a six, she grabs the pencil and begins writing from 1 to 100—1, 2, 3, 4, 5, and so on. Meanwhile, the die is passed from player to player as before, each trying to roll a six. The writer's goal is to reach 100 before another player rolls a six, grabs the pencil from the first writer, and starts furiously scribbling numbers himself. Speed, of course, is of the essence with both the number-writing and die-rolling—and the intensity builds as players get closer and closer to 100 before they're robbed of the pencil. First player to reach 100 wins. *Grant Sawatzky*

Personality Pursuit

Before you play this game, have 200 to 300 small strips of paper prepared. When the kids arrive, have them write on each strip a person's name—use the name of others in your group, celebrities' names, names of people dead or alive, comic strip characters, etc., just as long as the name is well-known to most of the group. Don't worry if names are written more than once—it makes the game more fun. Then put all these strips in a pail or box.

Now divide into two teams. A player from team A dips into the pail, grabs a name, and has 30 seconds to give clues to her teammates until they can guess the name. Any verbal clue is permissible—even pointing is allowed. If her team guesses the name within 30 seconds, that strip is pocketed by the team for scoring later; if the team fails to guess the name, the strip goes back into the bucket. Then team B follows suit. Make sure clue-givers are rotated each turn.

At the end of a designated time, each team tallies up the names it's guessed, and the team with the most wins. *Pete Kenow*

Movie Madness

Distribute one 3x5-inch card to each teenager and instruct kids to write down the name of a movie, TV program, or commercial. Players should not see what others have written. Collect the cards.

Now divide the group into teams of four or five each (involve the adult sponsors, too) and have each team draw one card from the pile you're holding. Teams then take three to five minutes to plan a scene from the movie, TV program, or commercial that they chose. After you've gathered the groups together again, let the team act out its scenes one at a time. The other teams can guess what movie, program, or commercial the performing team is portraying only when the performing team is finished.

For extra fun, record the evening on video—then edit it and play it at your next Movie Night. *David Smith*

License Plates

Here's a variation of a time-honored road game that just about everyone's played. Divide your group into teams, then hand out copies of page 107—one copy per team, or one copy per person. (For an easier game, use the matching version on page 108 instead.)

Give students a time limit to fill in (or match) the names of the 32 states. Here are the answers:

1. The Aloha State (Hawaii)
2. America's Dairyland (Wisconsin)

3. The Bay State (Massachusetts)
4. The Bluegrass State (Kentucky)
5. The Centennial State (Colorado)
6. The Constitution State (Connecticut)
7. The Empire State (New York)
8. First in Flight (North Carolina)
9. The First State (Delaware)
10. The Garden State (New Jersey)
11. The Golden State (California)
12. The Grand Canyon State (Arizona)
13. The Great Lake State (Michigan)
14. The Hawkeye State (Iowa)
15. The Heart of Dixie (Alabama)
16. The Hoosier State (Indiana)
17. The Keystone State (Pennsylvania)
18. Land of 10,000 Lakes (Minnesota)
19. The Land of Enchantment (New Mexico)
20. Land of Lincoln (Illinois)
21. Land of Opportunity (Arkansas)
22. The Lone Star State (Texas)
23. The Magnolia State (Mississippi)
24. The Ocean State (Rhode Island)
25. The Peach State (Georgia)
26. The Show-Me State (Missouri)
27. The Silver State (Nevada)
28. The Sportsman's State (Louisiana)
29. The Sunflower State (Kansas)
30. The Sunshine State (Florida)
31. The Vacation State (Maine)
32. The Volunteer State (Tennessee)
Bill Williamson

LICENSE PLATES

Fill in the blank with correct state name.

1. The Aloha State _____
2. America's Dairyland _____
3. The Bay State _____
4. The Bluegrass State _____
5. The Centennial State _____
6. The Constitution State _____
7. The Empire State _____
8. First in Flight _____
9. The First State _____
10. The Garden State _____
11. The Golden State _____
12. The Grand Canyon State _____
13. The Great Lake State _____
14. The Hawkeye State _____
15. The Heart of Dixie _____
16. The Hoosier State _____
17. The Keystone State _____
18. Land of 10,000 Lakes _____
19. The Land of Enchantment _____
20. Land of Lincoln _____
21. Land of Opportunity _____
22. The Lone Star State _____
23. The Magnolia State _____
24. The Ocean State _____
25. The Peach State _____
26. The Show-Me State _____
27. The Silver State _____
28. The Sportsman's State _____
29. The Sunflower State _____
30. The Sunshine State _____
31. The Vacation State _____
32. The Volunteer State _____

LICENSE PLATES

Match the state with the license plate phrase by writing the
name of the state on the appropriate line.

1. The Aloha State _____   Alabama
2. America's Dairyland _____   Arizona
3. The Bay State _____   Arkansas
4. The Bluegrass State _____   California
5. The Centennial State _____   Colorado
6. The Constitution State _____   Connecticut
7. The Empire State _____   Delaware
8. First in Flight _____   Florida
9. The First State _____   Georgia
10. The Garden State _____   Hawaii
11. The Golden State _____   Illinois
12. The Grand Canyon State _____   Indiana
13. The Great Lake State _____   Iowa
14. The Hawkeye State _____   Kansas
15. The Heart of Dixie _____   Kentucky
16. The Hoosier State _____   Louisiana
17. The Keystone State _____   Maine
18. Land of 10,000 Lakes _____   Massachusetts
19. The Land of Enchantment _____   Michigan
20. Land of Lincoln _____   Minnesota
21. Land of Opportunity _____   Mississippi
22. The Lone Star State _____   Missouri
23. The Magnolia State _____   Nevada
24. The Ocean State _____   New Jersey
25. The Peach State _____   New Mexico
26. The Show-Me State _____   New York
27. The Silver State _____   North Carolina
28. The Sportsman's State _____   Rhode Island
29. The Sunflower State _____   Pennsylvania
30. The Sunshine State _____   Tennessee
31. The Vacation State _____   Texas
32. The Volunteer State _____   Wisconsin

Up Jenkins

This game of concealment and feint is best played by small, even groups of six to 12 players. All that's needed is a long table, chairs for all players, and a quarter. Divide people into two teams; teams sit on opposite sides of the table. Each team elects a captain.

The game begins with one team secretly passing the quarter back and forth among its players underneath the table. When the captain of the opposing teams says "Up Jenkins!" all the players on the quarter-passing team close their fists, lift their arms, and place their elbows on the table. In one of the fists, of course, is the quarter. Then the opposing captain says "Down Jenkins!" and all the players simultaneously slam their hands down on the table. If it's done well, the other team won't be able to hear the quarter.

The object then is for the guessing team to eliminate all the hands that do not have the quarter, leaving at last the one hand with the quarter under it. So the opposing captain chooses people to lift a hand, one hand at a time. The team with the quarter can respond to the captain only; lifting a hand in response to anyone else on the opposing team means forfeiture of the quarter. One of the goals of the opposing team, therefore, is to persuade people to lift their hands in response to someone other than their captain. If the opposing team's captain successfully lifts all the hands except the one covering the quarter, his or her team wins and takes possession of the quarter. If, however, the captain uncovers the quarter before the last hand, the quarter-passing team retains possession and a new round begins.

Once the kids get the hang of it, they'll develop all sorts of strategies—how to make your hand "look guilty" when you don't have the quarter, etc. *Dave Sherwood*

Pucks And Pigskins

Time to put all your sports-spectating prowess to work. The object of the quizzes on pages 111 & 112 (Touchdown! and On Ice!) is to identify the football teams and the hockey teams from the clues. It's especially fun to play during half-time when your group is watching a televised sporting event together.

The answers:

TOUCHDOWN!

1. Dallas Cowboys
2. Washington Redskins
3. Philadelphia Eagles
4. Arizona Cardinals
5. New York Giants
6. Minnesota Vikings
7. Chicago Bears
8. Green Bay Packers
9. Detroit Lions
10. Tampa Bay Buccaneers

11. San Francisco 49ers
12. New Orleans Saints
13. Atlanta Falcons
14. St. Louis Rams
15. Miami Dolphins
16. Indianapolis Colts
17. New England Patriots
18. New York Jets
19. Buffalo Bills
20. Pittsburgh Steelers

21. Houston Oilers
22. Baltimore Ravens
23. Cincinnati Bengals
24. Oakland Raiders
25. Denver Broncos
26. Seattle Seahawks
27. Kansas City Chiefs
28. San Diego Chargers
29. Jacksonville Jaguars
30. Carolina Panthers

Play it!

ON ICE!

1. Pittsburgh Penguins
2. Hartford Whalers
3. Buffalo Sabres
4. Florida Panthers
5. Anaheim Mighty Ducks
6. Philadelphia Flyers
7. Montreal Canadiens
8. Detroit Red Wings
9. Calgary Flames

10. St. Louis Blues
11. New York Islanders
12. New York Rangers
13. Toronto Maple Leafs
14. Edmonton Oilers
15. Boston Bruins
16. Dallas Stars
17. Los Angeles Kings
18. Washington Capitals

19. Vancouver Canucks
20. Chicago Black Hawks
21. New Jersey Devils
22. Colorado Avalanche
23. San Jose Sharks
24. Phoenix Coyotes
25. Tampa Bay Lightning
26. Ottawa Senators

Phil Rankin and Terry H. Erwin

WRDS

The imaginations, vocabulary, and teamwork of your youth group will get a workout with this one. Give each team a list with several letter combinations on it—PMR, for example, and RTS and SPF. Each team attempts to make a word that keeps the letters in their order. From PMR a team might make ProMpteR; from RTS, ReTreatS. The team with the longest word wins that round—ReTreatS, for example, beats CRYing.

The winner of the most rounds wins the game. Variations? Require that words be proper nouns, foreign words, biblical words, etc. *Tim Gerarden*

TOUCHDOWN!

Can you recall which NFL teams go with the following clues?

1. Ranch hands
2. Cherokee, Navajo, Blackfoot, etc.
3. Bald birds
4. Catholic officials
5. Goliaths
6. Eric the Red's crew
7. Koala, grizzly, panda, etc.
8. Suitcase stuffers
9. Kings of the beasts
10. Pirates
11. Gold diggers
12. Holy ones
13. Swift birds of prey
14. Head bashers
15. Small whales
16. Young horses
17. Minutemen
18. F-15s
19. William Cody namesakes
20. Ironmen
21. Fossil drillers
22. Black crow cousin
23. India's cats
24. Vandals
25. Rodeo mounts
26. Aquatic fliers
27. Indian leaders
28. The electric company
29. Large tawny, spotted felines
30. Solid black leopards

ON ICE!

Come on, all you hockey jocks.
See how many NHL teams you
can name from these clues.
And remember—no high-sticking!

_____ 1. Birds in tuxedos
_____ 2. "A _____ of a time!"
_____ 3. These are "lite" swords
_____ 4. Black cats
_____ 5. Quack, quack
_____ 6. Frequent ones receive bonus mileage
_____ 7. These guys are from the Great White North
_____ 8. Embarrassed parts of a bird
_____ 9. On fire and all ablaze
_____ 10. "You got me singing the _____"
_____ 11. Remote inhabitants, much like Gilligan
_____ 12. Forest police
_____ 13. Falling from a syrupy tree
_____ 14. Well-drilled wells, not for water
_____ 15. Name of the bear in Reynard the Fox
_____ 16. "Twinkle, twinkle, little _____"
_____ 17. Ten, jack, queen, _____
_____ 18. This is a great kind of idea
_____ 19. French Canadian or Canadian French
_____ 20. A dark bird of prey
_____ 21. The fallen angel
_____ 22. Sliding snow
_____ 23. Jaws
_____ 24. Wile E. _____
_____ 25. _____ strikes
_____ 26. Elected representatives

Resources from Youth Specialties

Youth Ministry Programming

Camps, Retreats, Missions, & Service Ideas (Ideas Library)
Compassionate Kids: Practical Ways to Involve Your Students in Mission and Service
Creative Bible Lessons from the Old Testament
Creative Bible Lessons in 1 & 2 Corinthians
Creative Bible Lessons in John: Encounters with Jesus
Creative Bible Lessons in Romans: Faith on Fire!
Creative Bible Lessons on the Life of Christ
Creative Bible Lessons in Psalms
Creative Junior High Programs from A to Z, Vol. 1 (A-M)
Creative Junior High Programs from A to Z, Vol. 2 (N-Z)
Creative Meetings, Bible Lessons, & Worship Ideas (Ideas Library)
Crowd Breakers & Mixers (Ideas Library)
Downloading the Bible Leader's Guide
Drama, Skits, & Sketches (Ideas Library)
Drama, Skits, & Sketches 2 (Ideas Library)
Dramatic Pauses
Everyday Object Lessons
Games (Ideas Library)
Games 2 (Ideas Library)
Good Sex: A Whole-Person Approach to Teenage Sexuality and God
Great Fundraising Ideas for Youth Groups
More Great Fundraising Ideas for Youth Groups
Great Retreats for Youth Groups
Holiday Ideas (Ideas Library)
Hot Illustrations for Youth Talks
More Hot Illustrations for Youth Talks
Still More Hot Illustrations for Youth Talks
Ideas Library on CD-ROM
Incredible Questionnaires for Youth Ministry

Junior High Game Nights
More Junior High Game Nights
Kickstarters: 101 Ingenious Intros to Just about Any Bible Lesson
Live the Life! Student Evangelism Training Kit
Memory Makers
The Next Level Leader's Guide
Play It! Over 150 Great Games for Youth Groups
Roaring Lambs
Special Events (Ideas Library)
Spontaneous Melodramas
Student Leadership Training Manual
Student Underground: An Event Curriculum on the Persecuted Church
Super Sketches for Youth Ministry
Talking the Walk
Teaching the Bible Creatively
Videos That Teach
What Would Jesus Do? Youth Leader's Kit
Wild Truth Bible Lessons
Wild Truth Bible Lessons 2
Wild Truth Bible Lessons—Pictures of God
Worship Services for Youth Groups

Professional Resources

Administration, Publicity, & Fundraising (Ideas Library)
Equipped to Serve: Volunteer Youth Worker Training Course
Help! I'm a Junior High Youth Worker!
Help! I'm a Small-Group Leader!
Help! I'm a Sunday School Teacher!
Help! I'm a Volunteer Youth Worker!
How to Expand Your Youth Ministry
How to Speak to Youth...and Keep Them Awake at the Same Time
Junior High Ministry (Updated & Expanded)
The Ministry of Nurture: A Youth Worker's Guide to Discipling Teenagers

Purpose-Driven Youth Ministry Training Kit
So That's Why I Keep Doing This!
52 Devotional Stories for Youth Workers
A Youth Ministry Crash Course
The Youth Worker's Handbook to Family
Ministry

Discussion Starters
Discussion & Lesson Starters (Ideas Library)
Discussion & Lesson Starters 2 (Ideas Library)
EdgeTV
Get 'Em Talking
Keep 'Em Talking!
High School TalkSheets
More High School TalkSheets
High School TalkSheets: Psalms and Proverbs
Junior High TalkSheets
More Junior High TalkSheets
Junior High TalkSheets: Psalms and Proverbs
Real Kids: Short Cuts
Real Kids: The Real Deal—on Friendship,
    Loneliness, Racism, & Suicide
Real Kids: The Real Deal—on Sexual
    Choices, Family Matters, & Loss
Real Kids: The Real Deal—on Stressing Out,
    Addictive Behavior, Great
    Comebacks, & Violence
Real Kids: Word on the Street
Unfinished Sentences: 450 Tantalizing
    Statement-Starters to Get Teenagers
    Talking & Thinking
What If...? 450 Thought-Provoking Questions
    to Get Teenagers Talking, Laughing, and
    Thinking
Would You Rather...? 465 Provocative
    Questions to Get Teenagers Talking
Have You Ever...? 450 Intriguing Questions
    Guaranteed to Get Teenagers Talking

Art Source Clip Art
Stark Raving Clip Art (print)
Youth Group Activities (print)
Symbols, Phrases, and Oddities (print)
Clip Art Library Version 2.0 (CD-ROM)

Digital Resources
Clip Art Library Version 2.0 (CD-ROM)
Ideas Library on CD-ROM

Videos & Video Curricula
EdgeTV
Equipped to Serve: Volunteer Youth Worker
    Training Course
The Heart of Youth Ministry: A Morning with
    Mike Yaconelli
Good Sex: A Whole-Person Approach to
    Teenage Sexuality and God
Live the Life! Student Evangelism
    Training Kit
Purpose-Driven Youth Ministry
    Training Kit
Real Kids: Short Cuts
Real Kids: The Real Deal—on Friendship,
    Loneliness, Racism, & Suicide
Real Kids: The Real Deal—on Sexual
    Choices, Family Matters, & Loss
Real Kids: The Real Deal—on Stressing Out,
    Addictive Behavior, Great
    Comebacks, Violence
Real Kids: Word on the Street
Student Underground: An Event Curriculum
    on the Persecuted Church
Understanding Your Teenager
    Video Curriculum

Student Resources
Downloading the Bible: A Rough Guide to
    the New Testament
Downloading the Bible: A Rough Guide to
    the Old Testament
Grow For It Journal
Grow For It Journal through the Scriptures
Spiritual Challenge Journal: The Next Level
Teen Devotional Bible
What Would Jesus Do? Spiritual
    Challenge Journal
Wild Truth Journal for Junior Highers
Wild Truth Journal—Pictures of God